# Voodoo

*Unlocking the Hidden Power of Haitian
Vodou and New Orleans Voodoo*

# Your Free Gift (only available for a limited time)

Thanks for getting this book! If you want to learn more about various spirituality topics, then join Mari Silva's community and get a free guided meditation MP3 for awakening your third eye. This guided meditation mp3 is designed to open and strengthen ones third eye so you can experience a higher state of consciousness. Simply visit the link below the image to get started.

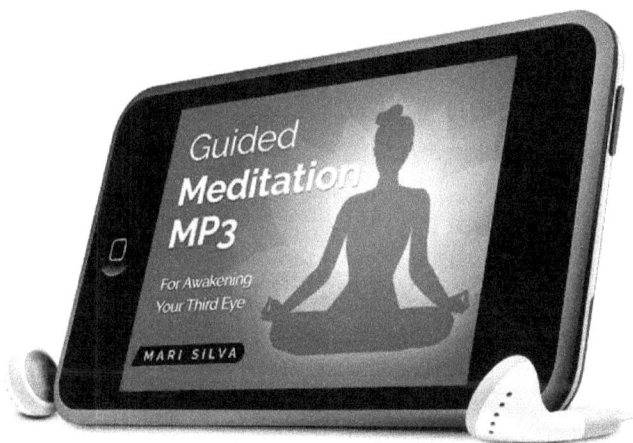

https://spiritualityspot.com/meditation

# Contents

# Introduction

What comes into your mind when you hear about Voodoo and its spells? Are you one of those who believe that it is a depiction of dark witchcraft or black magic that can harm someone? Then it is time to those misconceptions! Note that while it has garnered a bad reputation due to its portrayal in pop culture, it is not as evil as most people have claimed it to be.

To know more about Voodoo, you should open yourself up to the truth; it is inaccurate to describe it as just *dark magic*. It is not all about working with the devil and evil spirits to trigger harm to someone. Contrary to how the movies and TV shows present it, you can't tie it to evil's diabolical acts, puppets, and zombies.

Voodoo is more than those evil misrepresentations and misconceptions; it is a religion with deep roots. Voodoo practitioners place this religion in high regard. The practice is important to them, and they do not look at it as an instrument for torture, cannibalism, and devil worship.

To finally unlock the real power of Voodoo, rather than the historical misunderstandings and misrepresentations surrounding it, then this book will serve as your ultimate source of information. It is up-to-date and aims to correct all the misinformation and misconceptions about this specific religion that many practitioners love.

The good thing about this book is that it contains information that is easy to absorb and understand. Even beginners and those who are unfamiliar with Voodoo can quickly grasp the concepts. To learn more about Voodoo spells, you can also refer to this book as its steps and instructions are simple and easy to apply. By the time you have reached the end of this book, you will understand Voodoo's secrets and correct the misconceptions others strongly believe in. Now, let's begin your journey toward learning more about Voodoo and unraveling its secrets!

# Chapter 1: The Voodoo Twins - Haiti and New Orleans

Voodoo refers to a monotheistic and syncretic religion, which resulted from the combined religions of the native Africans and Roman Catholics. Mainly practiced in New Orleans and Haiti, you can see Voodoo being recognized in other locations, too, particularly in the Caribbean.

*Voodoo* has several definitions. The most socially acceptable and common one is that it is the act of worshipping more than just one God. It also worships spirits, ancestors, saints, and angels. This practice combines Catholic saint worship, witchcraft, Native American practices, and folk magic.

Contrary to what most people believe, Voodoo does not solely revolve around dark witchcraft and black magic to harm people. Most of the real practitioners of Voodoo state you can't do evil spirit worship here. So, it is time to finally set the record straight and understand that this practice is not as evil as others have claimed and believed it to be.

The spells associated with Voodoo are useful, powerful, and authentic. You can expect them to work effectively in various circumstances – among them are in the fields of finances, career, relationships, and love. However, it is safe to say that this religion has extensive coverage. Provided you use and practice it correctly, you can improve various aspects of yourself and your life through it.

# How Voodoo Started

The original roots of Voodoo can be traced back to Africa. It was brought to America by the African slaves after they were sold to white slave traders. Specifically, Voodoo started after the slaves in Africa carried their native traditions upon their forceful transport to the New World.

During that time, they were prohibited from practicing their faith and religion. With the restrictions and prohibitions set in place, these African slaves began equating the Gods they knew with the saints recognized in the Roman Catholic Church. They did that to sidestep the restrictions associated with the practice of their religions.

It also prompted them to do rituals with the help of the imagery and items used by and recognized in the Catholic Church. They incorporated the beliefs of the Catholics into their religious practices. Most believed it was the only way for them to continue practicing what they initially believed in. After all, restrictions meant they had to hide their former religious practices. They also did that because Voodoo naturally allowed them to incorporate saints into their practice.

When African slaves were moved to the New World, it was one of the darkest periods in world history. It was also when Voodoo contributed to helping everyone feel what it was like to be free – even if they did not have the right to practice freedom yet.

# African Voodoo

Of course, you would not completely understand Voodoo if you do not dig deeper into its roots. As mentioned earlier, this practice started in Africa. It began in Fon and Kongo, known as African kingdoms, around six thousand years back. The term, *Voodoo*, was even derived from the Fon language. It means *deity, spirit, or sacred.*

Presently, Fon is part of Southern Benin, a region referred to by many anthropologists as Voodoo's cradle. Millions of people continue practicing Voodoo even today, especially in Ghana, Togo, and other Northwestern African countries.

Voodoo is mainly an oral tradition. With that in mind, you will notice several differences and changes in the names of gods and the specific ways rituals are performed in various regions and generations. African Voodoo, however, demonstrates a few consistent qualities regardless of where it is practiced.

Aside from believing in spiritual possession and several gods, African Voodoo also differs. It consistently venerates or worships ancestors, using particular objects or rituals to spread magical protection. It also offers animal sacrifices to show respect to a god, ask for favors, or show their gratitude.

Africans also practice Voodoo by using fetishes and certain items with the power or essence of specific spirits. Ceremonial instruments, music, and dances that use elaborate masks and costumes are common in African Voodoo practice. Moreover, they do divination by interpreting physical activities.

You can also see most of its practitioners associating foods, colors, plants, and other objects, with a certain Loa, a Voodoo spirit designed to offer guidance in various aspects of life, like spirituality, healing, protection, success, sexuality, and death.

Most qualities and traits mentioned, especially those related to polytheism, ancestor worship, and dance and music, are also vital aspects of other religions practiced in Africa. With that in mind, you can look at Voodoo as similar to other traditional religions in the country.

Most observances also look like they are partly religious service and celebration with rhythmic music, songs, and dances. Several rituals performed in African Voodoo also use natural landscapes, including trees, mountains, and rivers.

African Voodoo turns the most mundane objects, such as bottles, pots, or slaughtered animals' body parts, into something sacred they can use in rituals. This is possible through the consecration and decoration of the said objects.

# Introduction to Voodoo's Most Important Branches

Now that you know how Africans practice Voodoo, it is time to know more about the two most important branches – the Haiti Vodou and the New Orleans Voodoo. The two branches were derived from a religious belief brought to America by the African slaves, so you can expect them to be similar.

It is still crucial to understand each branch separately, so you have a clear idea of what makes the two similar and different and how both originated.

## The Haitian Vodou

Haitian Vodou started around the 16th and 19th centuries. It was developed in Afro-Haitian communities when the Atlantic slave trade occurred during those times. It began after combining traditional religions carried by the slaves in West Africa to the Hispaniola Island with the teachings spread by French colonialists regarding the Roman

Catholic religion. The French colonialists had full control of the island.

Many of those who practiced Vodou participated in the Haitian Revolution that occurred between 1791 and 1804. It was when they contributed to conquering the government ruled by the French colonialists. It also contributed to abolishing slavery and the founding of what we can view as modern-day Haiti.

When they were still slaves, a code prevented them from practicing the religion they usually practiced. The slave code even required them to convert into Christians. This prompted them to get forcefully baptized as Christians, hugely influencing how they practiced Vodou.

The fact that the slaves were prohibited from observing and practicing their religion freely and openly caused them to borrow several elements of the Roman Catholics as a means of protecting their spiritual beliefs and practices. It resulted in the execution of the syncretization process, which had a major impact on the practice of Voodoo in Haiti.

After the Haitian Revolution, the church governed by the Roman Catholics also left the island. For a few decades, the absence of Catholics resulted in Vodou turning into Haiti's most dominant religion. During the 20th century, the increasing emigration rate caused Vodou to spread to other parts of the world.

In the latter part of the 20th century, people noticed a significantly growing connection between Vodou and some relevant traditions in the Americas, like Brazilian Candomblé and Cuban Santeria, and traditions practiced in West Africa.

# Common Beliefs in Haitian Vodou

One thing noticeable about Haitian Vodou is that it has no central institutional authority and liturgy. It also has communal and domestic variations. You will notice several variations in this community, particularly in its manner of practice in urban and rural areas and how it is executed in Haiti and in the global Haitian diaspora.

You will also notice variations in beliefs and practices from one congregation to another. One variation would be an extended family being a significant component of a single congregation. Other common beliefs of Haitian Vodou include:

### Bondyé and Loa (Lwa)

Haitian Vodou is mainly a monotheistic religion as it teaches the presence and existence of only one supreme God. This supreme entity built the universe, which Vodou practitioners recognize as Bondyé. Most practitioners also call Bondyé being transcendent and remote, a God who does not want to get involved in the everyday affairs of humans.

With that in mind, they also believe there is no point in directly approaching Bondyé. Instead, what Haitians often do is state "si Bondyé vie," which means "if Bondyé is willing" in their rituals. This is to signify their firm belief that everything will take place based on the will of the deity rather than on their needs expressed through prayer.

Vodou is also recognized as a polytheistic religion, teaching practitioners that a Loa (Lwa), a pantheon of deities, exists. This term refers to spirits, geniuses, or Gods that most Haitian Vodou practitioners believe in. There are also instances when Lwa's are viewed as the counterparts of angels in Christian cosmology. With that, they can offer protection, advice or counsel, and help to humans, provided they participate in ritual services.

All Vodou practitioners also regard Lwa as Bondyé's intermediaries – with each one of them displaying a unique personality. They also associate or link each Lwa to a specific color, object, and day of the week.

## Other Famous Beliefs

Haitian Vodou also believes in ethics and morality and that every gender has unique and different roles to play. Being a recognized religion, it mirrors the daily concerns of people. It also focuses on providing techniques that will help mitigate misfortunes and illnesses. Practitioners also believe those who do everything to survive are among the most highly ethical people.

In terms of morality, you will notice that Haitian Vodou does not implement too many rules. This means that the morality in this religion is not solely based on rules, but rather it is contextual based on the situation and the person subjected to it. According to Haitian Vodou followers, they consider someone as morally upright if he lives in accordance with his real character and the tutelary Loa (Lwa).

Aside from that, they put a lot of emphasis on conformity, support, group cohesion, and uniformity. The religion tries to strengthen family ties. They also emphasize showing respect to the elderly and view the extended family as a highly vital part of Haitian society. Most followers and practitioners of the religion do not also tolerate Maji, the term used to describe the process of using supernatural powers for evil and self-serving purposes.

## Common Practices

Haitian Vodou can be viewed as a religion composed of influences derived from several other religions. Despite the numerous obvious additions and integrations, Haitian Voodoo still strongly resembles the Voodoo practiced initially in Africa. For instance, they have designations for those who will carry out religious services and activities and offer traditional folk remedies, namely the houngans (priests) and mambos (priestesses).

Anyone who intends to serve as a houngan (or mambo) needs to participate in an apprenticeship program. They have to act as initiates with other recognized leaders in the community instead of just participating in a worship center. There is also what is referred to as *honfour* in Voodoo, which is where ceremonies occur. It is, therefore, the counterpart of a sanctuary or temple in other religions.

Aside from that, there are also other aspects of Haitian Voodoo that make their practice more recognizable. These include:

• **Spiritual Possession** - Similar to the Voodoo practiced in Africa, Haitian Voodoo also considers possession one of its most vital aspects. Practitioners refer to a person possessed as a horse with the possessing Lwa riding on it. One thing that helps them identify the possessed is when he/she has unnatural movements, speaks using unknown/unfamiliar languages, or delivers direct and clear statements to others who practice and follow the religion.

• **Sacrifice and Offerings** – Another element you will most commonly see in Haitian Voodoo is sacrifice. You can see them sacrificing animals, like chickens and goats, in various ceremonies. The reason is that Vodou strongly believes how important it is to feed the Loa (Lwa). Food offerings and drinks are just some rituals commonly practiced in the religion. They often do it at home or in communal spaces.

There is also a yearly feast (organized by a mambo or oungan) for the congregation, requiring congregants to sacrifice certain animals and offer them to the Lwa. Those who practice the religion also offer drinks and foods based on the exact Lwa they want to dedicate the feast or ritual to. Note that every Loa (Lwa) has different food preferences, so it is crucial to offer those they prefer during the ritual.

For instance, Danbala prefers white foods, notably eggs. There is also a Lwa known as Legba who wants any food served to him, whether vegetables, tubers, or meat, to be grilled.

• **Ritual Objects and Clothing** – Haitian Voodoo also makes a point to include certain objects, decorations, and clothing in their rituals and celebrations. Most of these items are also used to show how they respect the Lwa. Several also use Kongo (medicine) packets to hold items and herbs with medicinal or healing properties.

Many worshippers bring drapo (flags) with them all the time to demonstrate their respect for the spirits. You will also notice many using and playing various drums, rattles, and bells to invoke and calling the Lwa.

Other ritual items and objects used by those who practice Haitian Voodoo are decorated bottles, calabashes usually filled with food offerings, and dolls. They often put these items on altars. A few of these objects are now major components of Haitian crafts and artworks.

• **Altars and Shrines** – Haitian Vodou followers also practice their faith and belief with altars and shrines. Several altars even hold lithographs of saints recognized in the Roman Catholic religion. During the time chromolithography was developed, it immediately influenced the imagery used in Vodou. It resulted in the widespread access of images of saints derived from the Roman Catholic Church with their corresponding Loa (Lwa).

Vodou practitioners also made it a point to use various materials available to them to make shrines. There are also certain places, aside from the temples, that practitioners used when performing rituals. For instance, they often perform rituals in cemeteries, making the perfect place for rituals, particularly for those who want to approach and talk to dead spirits.

Many practitioners also choose crossroads as the perfect spot for rituals. The reason is that these are points that provide access to the world of the spirits. It is also possible to use Christian churches, markets, fields, the sea, and rivers for a Vodou ritual.

• **Healing** – Healing is also a common and essential practice in Vodou. The practitioners usually receive amulets and charms from oungan and Mambo. Also known as pwen or points, these charms and amulets are often based on plants known for their healing powers.

Usually a bath, which uses various ingredients that aid in healing, will be prescribed. Haiti also has several herb doctors offering herbal remedies to treat a wide range of ailments. However, these herb doctors are different as mambo and oungan, so expect certain limitations regarding the issues they can heal or handle.

• **Pilgrimage and Festivals** – Haitian Vodou also practice celebrating birthdays for a specific Loa (Lwa). This regularly happens when the Roman Catholics hold the All Souls and All Saints days. These celebrations require them to dedicate special altars designed for the Lwa whose birthday they want to celebrate.

They also honor the dead by holding celebrations that are often conducted in Port au Prince's cemeteries. This celebration comes in a festival with participants dressing up in a way associated with death. Some outfits, therefore, are purple and black coats, sunglasses, top hats, and black veils.

You can also see pilgrimage being a significant part of the culture of Haitian Vodou. Those who undertake the Haitian pilgrimage usually need to wear colored ropes around the waist or head.

Voodoo has now become an integral part of several Haitians' daily lives and activities, as over half of the Haitian population practices this religion. It is also the reason it has a crucial role in the history of the place.

# The Louisiana (New Orleans Voodoo)

The second most important branch of Voodoo we have to talk about is the Louisiana Voodoo, otherwise called the *New Orleans Voodoo*. This specific branch refers to a collection of spiritual practices and beliefs all developed based on the traditions followed by the African diaspora within Louisiana.

This Voodoo can also be defined as the cultural variation of the Afro-American religion developed within the Creole, Spanish, and French-speaking Afro-American population in the state. Louisiana Voodoo is one out of the numerous African-based religion incarnations that came from West African Dahomeyan Vodun. It was synchronized with the Roman Catholic religion and the Francophone culture famous in South Louisiana due to the trade of slaves.

While many confuse Louisiana Voodoo with Haitian Vodou, they are different. The one from Louisiana emphasizes using Gris-gris, Hoodoo occult paraphernalia, snake deity or the Li Grand Zombi, and voodoo queens. Louisiana Voodoo even played a role in introducing gris-gris and voodoo dolls in America's culture.

# How did it Start?

New Orleans or Louisiana voodoo came because of the enslaved West Africans who made it a point to merge their religious practices and rituals with the local Roman Catholic population. One important fact about New Orleans or Louisiana voodoo is that it strongly connects with the spirits, ancestors, and nature.

Voodoo was bolstered even more after its followers, who escaped from Haitian Revolution in 1791, moved to New Orleans. During this time, those who practiced Voodoo in North American colonies lived more complicated lives. The French colonists implemented more aggressive measures to suppress their rituals and avoid future uprisings. This is mainly because it was said that the revolution started after a Vodou ritual triggered slaves to be possessed by a deity.

Unlike their time in Haiti, the slaves who moved to Louisiana were not aggressive or rebellious against their masters. What they did, instead, was use charms and amulets to make their everyday lives easier. These Voodoo practitioners and followers used these items primarily for protection, healing, and guidance. They also believed that the charms and amulets were among the things that connected them with the people they loved. There were also charms believed to hurt their enemies. These items are what they used when making curses.

The slaves continuing to practice Voodoo turned into an extremely important part of the New Orleans culture. You can even see voodoo kings and queens becoming political and spiritual figures of the 1800s New Orleans power. It also caused the spread of the religion in other places, like across the Mississippi Valley, that still reported famous voodoo ceremonies up to 1891.

# New Orleans (Louisiana Voodoo) Major Beliefs

One major belief linked to the New Orleans (Louisiana) Voodoo is there is only one God who will never interfere or intercede with people's lives. Most of them believe that the spirits can preside and interfere with one's life. New Orleans or Louisiana voodoo practitioners believe that the spiritual forces are either mischievous or kind and capable of shaping their daily lives by interceding and interfering with them.

With that, they strongly recognize the importance of connecting with spirits. They can do that through music, dance, and singing. It is also possible to establish a spiritual connection by using snakes that mainly represent Legba, the spiritual conduit to all the others. The Voodoo serpent symbolizes not only healing knowledge but also the strong connection between the Earth and Heaven.

Singing is also a vital part of performing voodoo rituals. Practitioners sing to show how they worship God and the spirits. Usually, you can witness them singing while also clapping, stomping their feet, and patting. Drum playing was also part of the ritual when they were still slaves, and they did that only during the public ceremony held in Congo Square every week.

The songs played in rituals often describe the unique personalities of each deity. They mention the deity names, their origins, likes and dislikes, strengths, weaknesses, and responsibilities. Several songs reflect the tunes used in the Roman Catholic Church, and there is a connection between the saints in that religion with the deities famous in Africa.

Aside from songs (music) and dance, New Orleans Voodoo also uses gris-gris dolls, talismans, and potions. You can still find these items in households and stores throughout the city. This reminds everyone of the fascination of New Orleans, with not only spirits but also mystery and magic.

They also practice Voodoo through spiritual baths, personal ceremonies, prayer, and readings. Nowadays, those who continue to practice it also believe that it is a significant help in curing anxiety, depression, loneliness, and addictions. Many also use it to offer help to the sick, hungry, and poor.

# Famous Characters in New Orleans Voodoo

New Orleans Voodoo also introduced a few of the most famous characters to the world. There are famous Voodoo queens who make up the religion's most influential female practitioners, and they are known for exercising their immense power in communities. These led the majority of ritual dances and ceremonial meetings.

Among the most powerful and famous names in New Orleans Voodoo are the following:

### Marie Laveau

Marie Laveau (1794 to 1881) was the most popular Voodoo queen during her time. Many even call her the most powerful and eminent of the many voodoo queens in New Orleans. Even the wealthiest people, planters, businessmen, lawyers, and politicians approached her to ask her advice. They asked for her opinions whenever they needed to decide on business-related and financial matters. Laveau also made it a point to help the enslaved and the poor.

Laveau was so powerful that she dominated even the other renowned leaders of Voodoo in New Orleans. She was also a devout Catholic, so she urged her people to participate in the Catholic mass celebration. With her strong influence, it was no longer surprising to witness Roman Catholic practices being adopted into Voodoo's belief system.

People also remember her for how she showed compassion for the poor and less fortunate. Besides that, it was discovered that she was fond of filling her home with images of the saints, candles, items, and altars designed to keep it protected from spirits.

Even up to the present, Voodoo practitioners recognize Laveau's role in the practice of their religion. As a matter of fact, her gravesite became a tourist attraction. Voodoo practitioners and believers even continue to send gifts to her gravesite. She continues to be a prominent figure in Louisiana Voodoo and a major part of the entire culture of New Orleans.

### Doctor John

If there is a famous queen in Voodoo, there is also Dr. John, who is the most popular king in New Orleans Voodoo. Born in Senegal, Dr. John was kidnapped and brought to Cuba as a slave. Later on, he moved to New Orleans, where he participated in the Voodoo community.

It was during this time when his skills in Voodoo's medicinal aspects were recognized. People saw him as an incredible healer. Many believed that he could resurrect even those dying patients through Voodoo rituals. He eventually became Marie Laveau's teacher and is recognized today as one of the most prominent leaders in Louisiana Voodoo.

# The Modern New Orleans Voodoo

At present, many still practice Voodoo in New Orleans. Practitioners do it mainly to offer their service to others. Many also perform Voodoo to influence life events as they connect to spirits and ancestors.

Usually, Voodoo practitioners hold rituals privately. You can also find a lot of places that provide ritual assistance and readings. New Orleans even has a formally established temple for Voodoo, the Voodoo Spiritual Temple, that you can find across Congo Square.

You can also find museums in the city where you can learn about New Orleans Voodoo history and their famous rituals, altars, and artifacts. Voodoo in the city was even commercialized during the early parts of the 21st century.

Commercial interests pursued the capitalization of the strong interest of people in this religion. You can even see shops selling gris-gris, powders, candles, and charms today that cater to the needs of practitioners and tourists who want to learn more about Voodoo.

# Chapter 2: Bondye and the Voodoo Gods

Like many other pagan spiritual and belief systems, Voodoo practitioners also believe in different deities, spirits, Gods, and various Divine aspects. The belief is often based on the worldview of the practitioners and worshippers. With its different regional strains, like Haitian, New Orleans, Hoodoo, and Mississippi Valley, you may find this practice confusing. Still, you can make it a lot easier to understand by looking closely at each system's fundamental principles.

One way to do that is to learn about the deities that the systems and strains have in common and the similar energies they share. An important fact about Voodoo that can help you understand it even better, despite its numerous variations, is that it is a monotheistic religion.

This means that its followers believe in just one god. It is where Bondye comes into the picture as He is the Supreme Being that the Voodoo practitioners firmly have faith in. While they interact and communicate more with Lwa (Loa) or the spirits, it is the good God, Bondye, that they consider holding the highest power in their spiritual realm.

For practitioners to practice Voodoo without worrying about acceptance by society, the deities and Lwa (spirits) related to the Christian and Catholic hierarchy have to be recognized. By doing that, it would appear that they are petitioning a specific saint known in the Catholic religion when they are, in fact, communicating with a Voodoo Pantheon member. This is understandable when you look into the history of slavery and the subterfuge used for slaves to continue their religious practices.

Some connections to the Roman Catholic saints are clear and obvious. One example is St. Patrick, known to be the saint who cast out the snakes of Ireland. This saint was linked to Dambulla, which is known as Lwa in Voodoo.

St. Peter and the Lwa Papa Legba are also connected, considering that the two were the trusted ones to hold keys. Similar to St. Peter, with the keys to both heaven and Hell, Papa Legba is the one you have to invoke to reach other Lwas.

# Bondye Is the Supreme Being

In the Voodoo religion, only one God is considered supreme, and that is Bondye. He is called the creator God you can easily recognize as part of the Voodoo religion. He is also the Pantheon's head. As the only supreme God, the Lwa (Loa) or spirits are answerable to Him. These spirits even need to act as intermediaries between this supreme God and humans.

With Bondye holding superior power among all the deities and spirits known in Voodoo, His existence is so profound that humans can't comprehend it. His name, Bondye, was derived from the French term "Bon Deu, which means "The Good God." He got such a title even if he has no evil counterpart in the realm of Vodou deities.

In Voodoo, you can measure a person's "good" based on how much their actions increase or reduce the power of Bondye. This means that prosperity, happiness, and freedom that make a community stronger while protecting life are good for mankind. Those that tend to destroy these things are considered bad.

Similar to the Abrahamic God in Jewish, Islamic, and Christian religions, Bondye is also remote. He is inaccessible, which is why your requests for help, development, and assistance, and your prayers, should not only be aimed at the other deities but also other aspects closely linked to the Earth plane.

It would be like directing your rituals and prayers, including the lighting of candles, to the involved saints with certain areas of influence. Following what the Voodoo practitioners believe in, Bondye is also known as the universe's superior principle.

Recognized as the creator God, He holds responsibility for maintaining human activity and universal order. This God is also recognized as the wholeness of the whole of humanity. It is from Him that all forms of life come. All human lives also belong to him.

## Voodoo and the Lwas

Loa or Lwas refer to the spirits recognized in both Louisiana and Haitian Voodoo. They are the ones that all Voodoo believers communicate and interact with. Also spelled as Loa, it encompasses the main spirits who form part of any Voodoo variation. The term was derived from *loi,* a French word, which means *law.* It got such a name because each spirit represents a law of the human condition or law of nature.

You can liken these spirits to the Yoruba religion's orishas and the similar new religious movements of the Afro-Caribbean. Lwa can also be differentiated from orishas because the former can't be categorized as deities but spirits, whether they originated from the divine or humans. Bondye created these spirits so that the living would receive help and assistance in their daily affairs.

Lwas serves as the intermediaries between Bondye and humanity, considering this supreme creator is recognized for being distant from the world and humanity. One thing to note about Lwas is that they are not like angels and saints you simply have to pray to; you must serve them.

Lwas are forces of nature, but you can also expect them to have their own personal mythologies and unique personalities. Each is distinct, so they have their individual likes and dislikes, particular modes of service, and unique sacred songs, rhythms, ritual symbols, and dances.

It is also through a particular Lwa that Bondye can manifest his will. They are spirits capable of manifesting as forces with a huge impact on people's everyday lives. Remembering that, you will notice Voodoo ceremonies mainly focus on Lwa instead of Bondye. Those who practice this religion offer something to the Lwas. Aside from that, these spirits usually possess practitioners, making it possible for them to interact and communicate directly with the community.

Sometimes, those who are unfamiliar with Voodoo refer to Lwas as Gods. This is a mistake, though. Remember that they are mainly spirits who serve as intermediaries between Bondye and the physical world.

## Venerating or Worshipping the Lwa

For most Voodoo practitioners and devotees, the Lwa has a major influence on their lives. They firmly believe that they have an intense and demanding but fulfilling relationship with the Lwa. As devotees, they offer their service to these spirits who they respect not only and love but also fear. They regard the Lwa with high respect.

One method of showing respect is adding the prefix Papa, which means father, Maman, which means mother, and Maitresse, which means mistress, whenever they refer to a Lwa. By showing their piety and devotion to the Lwa they believe in, they also expect to receive protection, favors, and blessings from them in return.

Voodoo practitioners also show their devotions and respect to the Lwas by holding ceremonies. During these ceremonies, they can show clearly how intense their relationship is to the Lwas they have faith in. These ceremonies equal religious services they often perform inside an ounfò with the Vodou houngan (priest) or mambo (priestess) facilitating them.

The place where the ceremony is held also comes with a peristyle, which is a semi-open space often situated at the entrance. The central part of it is where the practitioners perform their public rituals. You will also notice a pillar in the middle that features a beautifully designed spiraling snake. With this pillar, the ground gets connected to the ceiling.

It is in this pillar where the Lwa will either descend or ascend. With that, it is safe to say that this pillar, otherwise called *potomitan*, has a crucial role whenever Voodoo ceremonies occur. This pillar also has a strong connection with Papa Legba (the crossroads' keeper) and Danbala.

Each Voodoo ceremony, which aims to call upon a Lwa, involves a lot of dancing, songs, and music, spiritual drawings or vèvè tracing, and drumming, and prayers. These activities are meant to invite the Lwa to participate in the ceremony, join the living, and receive and accept any sacrifice or offering that the devotees present.

One sign of successfully calling upon a Lwa is when he/she arrives by riding on an attendee. This is usually the mambo or houngan who presides the religious service or ceremony. When this happens, the spirit will get the chance to communicate with those who are part of the ceremony. Here, the living may start presenting their requests and asking questions to the Lwa so they can take full advantage of the spirit's presence.

One fact about the Lwas you should know is that they showcase unique and distinctive behavior that makes them easily recognizable. Many even have specific actions and phrases you can immediately relate to them.

Once a Lwa gains recognition, the symbol dedicated explicitly to him will finally be given. For instance, there is this Lwa known as Erzulie Freda, who will only accept pink champagne. As for Papa Legba, the perfect gifts would be his cane, pipe, and straw.

# The Three Main Families of Lwa

As indicated earlier, Voodoo practitioners must serve and worship a pantheon of spirits known as the Lwa. In modern Voodoo, the Lwa of the spirits practitioners communicate their concerns to and regularly interact with are categorized into three major families/nations - the Rada, Petro, and the Ghede. Let's get to know more about each family and the spirits or Lwas belonging to each one.

# Rada Lwa Spirits

This family originated from Africa. It encompasses the deities and spirits that the slaves (taken to the New World) honored and respected, so they were the original Lwas. They turned into the primary spirits in the newly synthesized religion there. Most spirits who belong in this family are creative and benevolent. They are also primarily water spirits, which is why you can often see them served with water.

The Rada Lwa spirits are also recognized for their calm nature because they are less aggressive than the spirits and deities belonging to the Petro family. When serving Rada Lwas, it is crucial to remember that the most appropriate color is white. They also have stable personalities and are more likely to display a more defensive stance than an aggressive one.

Among the most prominent spirits or Lwas in the Rada family are:

## Papa Legba

The Voodoo religion views Papa Legba as its most important Lwa. Associated with crossroads, he acts as the gatekeeper, making it possible for Voodoo devotees and practitioners to interact and communicate with the spirit. As the crossroad deity, he has full control over the gate between the world of the living and the spiritual world.

Not surprisingly, people perceive him as the counterpart of St. Peter in Roman Catholic. Papa Legba has a strong connection with stray dogs and appears like an older man holding crutches. His symbols, therefore, include stray dogs, tobacco and pipe, and spiritual crossroads.

The most appropriate offerings for him are rum, tobacco, spiced chicken, and black-eyed peas. You may also want to offer sacrificial animals to him, mainly goats and roosters.

## Loko

Perceived as the patron of plants and healers, particularly the trees in Voodoo, Loko has a strong connection with the trees. He is the guardian of sanctuaries and the spirit of vegetation. He is capable of providing healing properties to leaves. Considered by many as the healing god, he is also a patron of most herb doctors. They often invoke this spirit whenever they need to undertake a treatment. They often put their offerings to him in a straw bag then hang them in the branches.

One recognizable feature of Loko is the stick that his hand carries. You can also recognize him through the pipe that his servant smoked. He likes the colors white and red the most. Therefore, some of the animal offerings appropriate for this spirit are white or black goats and russet-colored oxen.

Many also recognize Loko because of his excellent judgment. With that, it is no longer surprising to see him being called in to act as a judge whenever there are conflicts. He does not tolerate injustice. He can transform into the wind then listen to the living without their knowledge. His primary duties, though, will always be on wood and forest vegetation.

### Agwe

Agwe is also another famous Rada Lwa who is identified as the water spirit. With his water representation, it is no longer surprising to see seafarers interested in this Lwa. When performing ceremonies for him, it is advisable to do it close to the water. Some offerings that please him are white sheep, rum, gunfire, toy ships, and champagne.

You offer him these gifts by letting them float on the surface of the water. If the gifts or offerings go back to the shore, it means that Agwe refused them. As for the colors, the ones that represent him are usually white and blue. This Lwa is also linked to the Roman Catholic saint known as St. Ulrich. The reason is that St. Ulrich was seen holding a fish, so he has a strong connection with water.

### Damballah-Wedo

Damballah-Wedo is also another of the most crucial Lwas, particularly in New Orleans Voodoo and Haitian Vodou. This spirit has a strong connection with the act of creation as he was also the one who offered help to Bondye in creating the cosmos. Portrayed by a snake or giant serpent, you will notice him displaying the behavior of a snake whenever he possesses a human. This means that he does a lot of whistling and hissing instead of talking.

The coils of Damballah-Wedo, though, played a crucial role in shaping the earth and heavens. He holds a lot of healing magic, wisdom, and knowledge. He can move the sea and land and holds the constant force representing life's venerations. As a creator, he is known for being a loving father to everything he created.

The mere presence of this Lwa is enough to bring harmony and peace. He is a primary source of life with a strong connection with rain and water. There are a couple of saints linked to him in the Roman Catholic religion – one of which is St. Patrick, the one who had successfully driven the snakes away from Ireland.

Another prominent religious figure linked to him is Moses, with his staff transformed to a snake to prove how powerful God was. He likes the color white. As for the offerings, you can gift Damballah-Wedo with corn syrup, eggs mounted on top of flour, white objects, like white flowers, and chicken.

### Erzulie Freda

This Rada Lwa is recognized as the mistress ruling the realms of wealth and love. Voodoo practitioners and devotees may call or petition this Lwa to change their present financial conditions or add romance to their life. Take note, though, that the love that Erzulie brings does not usually last. The reason is that she tends to focus more on the brief yet erotic and passionate affairs of the ones seeking her help.

Erzulie Freda is also known for her passion, capriciousness, volatility, and flirtatious nature. The colors representing her include light blue and pink. Offerings she loves include flowers, white doves, perfume, sweet cakes, and champagne.

One thing to note about Erzulie is that she cries whenever she successfully possesses a devotee or practitioner during a ceremony or ritual because she often ends up unsatisfied with even the most luxurious items offered to her. She is the counterpart of Mater Dolorosa in the Roman Catholic faith.

# Petro Lwa Spirits

The spirits or Lwas in the Petro family came from the New World, more specifically from modern Haiti. However, you can't find the Lwas or spirits here in the practice of African Vodou.

Usually, this family consists of spirits naturally more aggressive compared to other families. They also are fiery and warlike. The spirits here also have darker personalities than Rada's, but you can't categorize the two families into good and evil right away. If you do that, then there is a risk of misrepresentation, causing the rituals designed for offering assistance or causing harm to involve just one of them.

Instead, remember that even Rada Lwas, who seem to be all-white and pure, also have Petro counterparts in them. This means they also have their aggressive and dark side, though not as imminent as the ones in Petro. In other words, while Rada spirits are often perceived as benign or peaceful, they can also make evil magic.

Petro spirits, on the other hand, despite their aggressive nature, also perform beneficial workings such as healing. However, you can accurately call both families hot and cool, respectively.

To get to know more about this family, here are the most recognized Lwas/spirits under Petro:

### Erzulie Dantor

Erzulie Dantor is the Petro side of Erzulie Freda. She is a vengeful and fiery spirit who came to life when practitioners struggled for independence. Many Voodoo practitioners invoke her to punish a lover who abused their partner or anyone who caused serious harm to their children.

Despite her harsh and wild nature, she still acts as a mother, a perfect one at that who genuinely cares for and watches her children. She is a disciplinarian and does not tolerate bad behaviors in children. Depicted as a loving and protective mother, you can associate her with

Our Lady of Mt. Carmel, Our Lady of Perpetual Help, and Our Lady of Lourdes. All of them are recognized in the Catholic religion.

One offering she will most likely accept is *kleren*, which refers to a fiery drink in a rum infused with hot peppers. She also likes to receive peas and rice as gifts. As for the animal you can offer to her as a sacrifice, the best one would be a wild Creole pig. She also likes everything that's either blood red or navy blue.

### Marinette

Another Lwa under the Petro family is Marinette. She is a Lwa of violence and power recognized in Haitian Vodou. Among all the Voodoo Lwas, she is considered the most dreaded one considering how powerful and cruel she is. The werewolves respect her. She does not like it when people burn humans and animals. These situations trigger her to become cruel, though she only shows her cruelty whenever she hates someone.

Another fact about Marinette you should know is that worshipping her is not a widespread practice in Haiti, though you can see her popularity rapidly growing in Southern areas. Her devotees hold ceremonies for her under a tent. It involves lighting it up with a big fire and throwing petrol and salt into the fire.

The ceremonial colors intended for Marinette include black and bloody red. She also likes it when Voodoo practitioners offer black roosters and black pigs plucked alive during ceremonies.

### Met Kalfu

Met Kalfu has traits and aspects opposite of Papa Legba. He also has control of the crossroads and is capable of granting or denying your access to other spirits or Lwas. Moreover, he allows bad luck, injustices, misfortunes, and deliberate destructions to cross. He is also linked to almost all evil forces existing in the world.

Many even consider Met Kalfu as a trickster and a life destroyer. With his negative reputation, he may not be the perfect spirit to seek help from at first. It would be much better to approach the Lwas in

Rada before approaching anyone from the Petro family. So, Met Kalfu is not the most suitable spirit for any witch to call on or summon haphazardly.

The bad reputation of Met Kalfu, combined with his being the dark version of Papa Legba, is why he is usually syncretized with Satan. He favors the color red and loves offerings in the form of rum infused with gunpowder.

# Ghede Lwa Spirits

The third family consisting of Lwas is known as Ghede. The spirits belonging to this family are the unremembered and unclaimed dead. Besides representing the dead spirits, it also symbolizes the process of death itself, which all Voodooists believe is a simple passage or transition from one state to another. This means that death is a scenario they should not fear.

As a family, the spirits under Ghede are considered rude and loud. The spirits here also transport the souls of the dead. They have irreverent behaviors and are usually the ones who make sexual or obscene jokes. They also do dances following the act of sexual intercourse. Aside from that, Ghede Lwas or spirits can celebrate life even if someone is already close to death. The traditional colors of this family include purple and black.

### Baron Samedi

He is one of the most prominent figures in the Voodoo religion. He is so prominent and influential that he leads the Guede family. He is the Lwa representing resurrection, gravestones, and graveyards. This spirit is usually chaotic and enjoys communicating with people. He also loves to smoke and drink.

One crucial fact about his personality you should know is that he is naturally morbid. He is wild, rowdy, and loud and loves to have a good time. Even if he drinks a lot and has an immense party lifestyle, this Ghede family leader still acts with style and class. He even guards and protects the dead.

Bardon Samedi is the counterpart of St. Martin de Porres. He is fond of the colors white, purple, and black. He likes to accept the gifts of rum, grilled peanuts, bread, cigars, and black coffee. Besides being the master of those already dead, Baron Samedi also acts as the giver of life. He is also the husband of Maman Brigitte.

### Maman Brigitte

For those who practice the New Orleans Voodoo and the Haitian Vodoun religion, Maman Brigette is a prominent Lwa. She is strongly connected with cemeteries and death, but many also view her as the primary spirit of motherhood and fertility. She is also an extremely important Lwa as she absorbs the beliefs of other cultures into Voodoo.

She is also a strong representation of the ideal female in the religion. Despite her motherly nature, Maman Brigitte is known for being protective, strong, and aggressive to where she can punish anyone who does not respect the dead. She punishes anyone who does not provide the dead with a proper burial.

Most practitioners and devotees of Voodoo also invoke her for luck whenever they gamble. Her favorite ceremonial colors are purple and black. As for the offerings, among her favorites are black roosters, rum infused with pepper, and candles. Mary Magdalen is her counterpart in the Roman Catholic religion as they have a few similarities as far as their image is concerned.

# The Mystic Marriage (Maryaj Mistik)

One more aspect about Lwas you have to learn involves the mystic marriage (Maryaj Mistik). It is an important aspect of the Lwas as it is a common occurrence among Vodou adherents, despite whether they have already undergone initiation. It happens as part of the ritual called the mystic marriage.

The entire ritual resembles an actual wedding ceremony conducted for two humans. This means it also requires the use of special attire and the presence of a priest, wedding ring, and wedding cake. The main goal of performing the mystic marriage is to build a special relationship with a Lwa, which is said to help in gaining more spiritual protection from them.

A taboo linked to this specific kind of marriage is the requirement to abstain from sex on any holiday-related to the Lwa. This is necessary to ensure that the practitioner or devotee to whom the Lwa gets married continues to receive the messages from their spiritual spouse. Such messages are often sent through dreams during the specific night when abstinence is a requirement.

Usually, practitioners or devotees choose to get married to their mèt tèt. This is the Lwa identified to walk with this person, whether or not through spiritual consultation or divination. In most cases, the devotee and their mèt tèt have a strong resemblance as far as their personalities are concerned. For instance, if you have Erzulie Freda as your mèt tèt, you can also have her personality, including being frivolous and generous.

# Chapter 3: Becoming a Vodouisant

To become a Voodooist or just learn their ways, then you should understand the shared beliefs of those who practice it. You have already had a glimpse of these beliefs in the first couple of chapters, but it is time to dig a little deeper. That way, you will know exactly how Voodoo is practiced and how you can do it independently.

## The Truth About Voodoo

Unlike the beliefs of many, the Voodoo community is not around to create zombies, summon evil spirits, and kill chickens and other animals for no reason. The Voodoo, necromantic, and nature spells are often done by Voodoo practitioners to serve, interact, and communicate with the powerful Lwas or spirits.

Similar to the Wicca religion, Voodoo is somewhat misunderstood. Several traditions and beliefs in Wicca and the Judeo-Christian faith are also part of the Voodoo community. With that in mind, Voodoo practitioners believe in celebrating important life events, such as births, deaths, and marriages. Those who are part of the Voodoo community believe in spirits (Lwas), and just one chief or supreme God also makes it resemble Christianity.

They also have their versions of priests and priestesses who contact Lwas whenever they perform long rituals. They are often the ones possessed or ridden by the spirits. Even if this form of possession has nothing to do with black magic, the untrained and unfamiliar may still look at it as an unsettling experience. So, only try to do complicated Voodoo spells once you have learned the most important facts and aspects.

# The Birth of Misconceptions

It is no longer a secret; there are a lot of misconceptions revolving around Voodoo. Most of these misconceptions originated from the book written by Sir Spenser St. John in 1884 entitled <u>Hayti: or the Black Republic</u>. It inaccurately described Voodoo, demonstrating it as an evil religion involving wicked acts like cannibalism and human sacrifices.

The way Voodoo was described and depicted in the book is terrifying that those who were not part of this community started to fear it. It caused misunderstandings about Voodoo to spread from that moment – and even up to today. The fear and misconceptions further increased as Hollywood also depicted and cast Voodoo in a bad and unfavorable light.

# Voodoo Beliefs and Christianity

The roots of Voodoo in Western Africa came from the ancient practices linked to animism and ancestor worship. This means they strongly believed that spirits could inhabit all things, such as plants and animals.

As has been indicated earlier, the practitioners and devotees of this religion also have strong faith in Bondye, the all-powerful and supreme God who stays detached from the affairs of humans.

Because of this God's detachment from humans, it has been the habit of practitioners to find help from their ancestors' spirits and the spirits of nature so they can find solutions to their problems.

Voodooists also believe that Lwas and humans have reciprocal relationships. They offer food and other possible gifts that the Lwa they are planning to reach out to will find appealing – so they can receive the spirit's help or assistance in return. During rituals, Lwas are often encouraged to possess believers and devotees present, allowing them to interact directly with the spirits.

Based on the community's beliefs, Voodoo and the Roman Catholic religions have a few similarities. Both religions are similar in the sense that their individual practitioners and devotees believe in:

- One Supreme Being
- The afterlife
- Ceremonies that require the consumption of body and blood
- Demons and evil spirits

Aside from that, Voodoos also believe in a *met tet*, which means master of the head. You can access this met tet within a Lwa. When compared to Christianity, the met tet is the counterpart of the patron saint. Lwas also resemble the saints in Christianity as they were once recognized as people who lived extraordinary and incredible lives. Like saints, deities also hold the unique attributes and responsibilities that all living beings should strive to follow.

The Lwas are also different from the saints in the Roman Catholic religion because some can be categorized as evil. For instance, there is an evil spirit in the Voodoo religion known as Baka, who can transform into an animal. Another evil Lwa (or spirit) in Voodoo is Kalfu, who controls the spiritual world's evil forces while also being closely linked to black magic.

Though, most spirits in Voodoo are good, which is why their attributes are shared with Christian saints. Voodoo practitioners also believe in Vilokan, the home of not only Lwas but also the deceased. This home is portrayed as a forested and submerged island with Papa Legba as its guard and protector. He is the one that the practitioners should appease before they can directly talk to any of the residents in the Vilokan.

# Rituals and Practices

Voodoo practitioners also strongly believe in the importance of regularly ritualizing to communicate with the spirits. In most cases, the rituals include these practices:

• **Animal Sacrifices** – As the name suggests, it involves sacrificing animals during the Voodoo rituals. Various animals may be killed and then offered; the sacrifices offered will greatly depend on the specific Lwa practitioners plan to address. These offerings aim to provide spiritual sustenance to the Lwa. The flesh of the offered animals, on the other hand, is usually cooked then eaten during the ritual by those who participated in it.

• **Veves** – The rituals also include the use of drawings displaying the specific symbols representing the Lwa. These symbols are referred to in the community as veves. All Lwas have their individual veves or symbols that the practitioners have to draw – or use to worship or summon the spirits.

• **Voodoo Dolls** – Most Voodooists also believe in the significant role played by Voodoo dolls during rituals. You should note that the usual perception of Voodoo practitioners poking pins into these dolls is not reflective of the traditional religion. What the practitioners and devotees do, instead, is dedicate these Voodoo dolls to a specific Lwa. They also use dolls to attract the influence of the spirit.

The rituals that every Voodooist does also often revolve around interacting with the Lwa. The ceremonies make use of the veves along with songs, dancing, drumming, and praying. They believe in the need to gather together to serve and commune with the Lwa. In most cases, the ceremonies they set for a specific Lwa also correspond with a Roman Catholic saint's feast day, particularly the saint to whom the Lwa is connected.

Aside from that, all Voodoo practitioners must master all forms of ritual. They have to constantly remind themselves of the primary purposes of rituals – one of which is healing things or *echofe*, which is the actual term used for this purpose in Voodoo. This means it aims to change something, whether facilitating the healing process or eliminating any barriers.

Another important belief in Voodoo as for performing rituals is the need to practice secrecy. Before the later parts of the 20th century, devotees practiced this religion secretly.

# The Soul

The Voodoo community also ingrains into the minds of its devotees and practitioners that a soul exists. This soul comes in two parts. The first one is the little good angel (ti bon ange), which refers to the conscience that makes one criticize and reflect on himself. The second one is the big, good angel (gros bon ange), which constitutes many vital aspects of a person, including his psyche, personhood, intelligence, and memory source.

Voodooists strongly believe these two essential parts of the soul live in one's head. The gros bon ange is also said to be capable of leaving your head and traveling even if you are sleeping or whenever a Lwa possesses you during a ceremony or ritual. According to Voodoo followers, there is a great chance for this specific part of your soul to get damaged. It may also be captured and attacked by evil magic at a time when it is no longer part of your body.

The two parts of the soul that the Voodooists believe in differ from the Catholic faith. The reason is that Roman Catholics believe there is only one soul. Despite that, the two religions continue to be the same because their beliefs include the possibility of evil possession. Both even perform an exorcism to eradicate the demon or evil person who entered or possessed someone.

Another important thing that the Voodooists believe regarding the soul is that the dead's spirits differ from the Guédé, whom they call Lwa. What makes them different is that the dead has to continue participating in the affairs of humans, particularly those who need sacrifices.

This specific belief makes it different from Christianity. Voodoo does not tell its practitioners there is an afterlife, which is part of Christians' beliefs regarding Heaven and Hell. In the Voodoo religion, the dead's spirits complain about being in a damp and cold realm that also causes them to experience hunger.

# The Priests (Houngan) and Priestesses (Mambo)

Like other religions, mainly Roman Catholic, the Voodoo community also has its version of the priests. Called houngan or oungan in the community, the male priests serve as the dominating figures in Voodoo. They also have female counterparts (the priestesses) known as mambo or mambo. Based on numbers, rural Haitian Vodou is dominated by the Houngan. But the urban areas seem to have an equal balance between the Houngan and mambo (priests and priestesses).

These dominant figures in the Voodoo community play a lot of essential roles – among which are:

- Organizing liturgies
- Using divination for client consultations

- Preparing initiation rituals
- Creating healing remedies for the sick

The Lwa itself determines those who can become a priest or priestess in Voodoo. According to the community's beliefs, the person destined to become either a houngan or mambo will just receive a calling from Lwa. If one gets the calling, he/she should avoid refusing it. The reason is that any refusal from the calling to become a priest or priestess can cause misfortune.

Voodoo practitioners believe that the houngan's roles resemble the ones represented by Loco, one of the most recognized Lwas. Loco, together with Ayizan, his consort, was the first to hold the titles houngan and mambo in the community, making them the first two sources of knowledge to the community.

As Voodoo's dominating figures, the houngan and mambo also need to demonstrate their clairvoyance or their second sight. It is a gift from the supreme creator, which the community members can only access through dreams or visions. These figures derived their primary income from the community services (for example, healing the sick and selling amulets and talismans they created themselves). This also means that the competition between them was a bit stiff.

There are even instances when they become richer than the people or clients they serve. Still, they continue to be among the most well-respected and influential members of the Voodoo community. Without them, Voodoo will cease to exist. With these priests and priestesses, the community's faith also revolves around two fundamentals: life has no accidents, and all things are connected.

It is similar to the beliefs of other religious sectors that humans are not independent and separate. They are part of a vast community with strong connections to each other. The priests here also teach Voodoo practitioners about the golden rule in life: avoid doing to others what you do not want to be done to you.

# The Voodoo Temples (Hounfo)

The *Hounfo* (or Voodoo temples) are also among the aspects of the community that the devotees firmly have faith in. This temple is the heart of most of their communal activities since this is where they undertake them. Note, though, that you can't find a single, uniform structure for this temple. Each varies in shape and size. You can find simple and basic shacks and more luxurious and lavish structures. The lavish ones are usually those that are in Port au Prince.

One thing to note about Hounfo or the Voodoo temples is that each has a unique design, greatly dependent on the taste and available resources of the priest or priestess running it. Each temple is also independent and unique so that you can see its unique customs and traditions.

In the Hounfo or temple, you will find the peristyle, which is considered the main space where the ceremonies occur. Here, you will find posts constructed from corrugated iron, with bright paintings, and these are used in holding up the roof. One post, specifically located at the center, is called the poto mitan, the one used as a pivot whenever they do ritual dances. The spirits or Lwas also pass through it every time there is a ceremony for them.

The Voodoo temple is also noticeable by the many sacred objects surrounding it. Here, you can find sacred items, like a black cross, iron bar, and pool of water. There are also sacred trees used to mark the temple's external boundary. A Hounfo with these sacred trees surrounding it also comes with other holy items hanging in them, including animal skulls and some strips of material.

You can also find different kinds of animals, including birds and a few mammals, like goats, inside the Hounfo's perimeters. The primary purpose of having these animals is to keep them handy whenever they need to use them for sacrifices during rituals.

The people gathering at the temple are the actual members of the spiritual group or community who seriously practice and believe in Voodoo. These members are called the children of the house or the pititt-caye. They worship the spirits in the temple using various forms of ritual and through the supervision and authority of the priests or houngan and the priestesses or mambo.

There is also what is called the *ounsi* in the community. It refers to those who are committed to offering their service to the Lwa for their entire lives. Males and females of the community can be an ounsi, but most are typically female. They hold several duties and responsibilities: offering animal sacrifices, participating in dances that require them to be fully prepared for the possible possession of a Lwa and keeping the peristyle clean.

For a Voodoo community member to become an ounsi, he/she has to go through the imitation ceremonies that the priests and priestesses will conduct. Here, the priests and priestesses will oversee and facilitate the entire training process. They also serve as healers, protectors, and counselors for the aspiring ounsi. With the many roles that they have to play to make the goal of the ounsi come to life, the latter must show their respect and obedience to the former in return.

An ounsi will also be tasked to act as the choir mistress or the hungenikon. The one assigned to this role will play the vital task of supervising the singing of the liturgy. He/she will also need to control the ceremony's rhythm helped by a cha-cha rattle that needs to be shaken constantly.

Another relevant figure in the group of ounsi is the confidant or *confiance*. This ounsi will be the one to supervise the administrative functions of the Voodoo temple (Hounfo). The ones initiated by the priests and priestesses will also be required to build or form families within the community.

Anyone interested in becoming part of the Voodoo community can participate in a specific Hounfo if it is present in the locality where he resides. If you have a relative who is already a community member, you can be part of the congregation, too. Suppose you want to offer your service on a specific Lwa. There, you can also find Voodoo temples devoted to such a spirit. It is also possible to be part of the congregation where the priest or priestess has left a good impression on you.

# The Initiation Rituals

Now it is time to know more about the initiation rituals you have to go through to become a Voodooist or a Voodoo devotee or practitioner yourself.

One crucial fact to remember is that there is a particular hierarchy in this community, which requires potential members to undergo a set of initiation rituals. Basically, it has multiple levels – the last of which allows one to hold the highest rank in the community, the houngan (priest) or mambo (priestess).

The initiation is usually a long process, mostly taking a couple of weeks. Basically, you must go through the initial rite, known as *kanzo*, first. Here, your main responsibility would be to participate in the first few ceremonies called *bat ge*, which means the act of beating a war. You will most likely encounter this during the initiation since you will be winning a battle to ensure that the aspiring voodooists will gain possession of the mysteries.

Each temple differs based on the number of nights they often spend performing the bat ge. Regardless of that number, the ritual's focus will usually be on a unique and distinctive Petro-based altar called a *bila*. One night of bat ge will also be dedicated to a ceremony called *pile fey*, which involves crushing herbs.

The crushed herbs will be used over the entire duration of the kanzo. You can expect these herbs to be empowered and charged specifically through the special ceremony. There will also be one night specifically dedicated to initiating the tie packets. This ceremony will require the participation of only the houngans and mambos.

After that, a series of special baths symbolizing the death of those intending to become voodooists will occur. Various Voodoo temples and houses differ in the number of days or times they perform these baths. Some do it for three days, while others complete the process within just one to two days. The number of baths that a candidate must take may differ based on the temple or house he is in.

As for the actual process, expect the candidate to be led in a procession first to reach the priest or priestess who will be the one to bathe them. Once done, he can rest for a bit while waiting for the following procedure he has to go through. The Kouche kanzo refers to secluding the initiate that may also involve a lot of dancing.

As part of the initiates, you will also need to feed Ayizan with sacred food. The whole ritual also involves setting up a special and distinctive throne for Ayizan. Here, you can expect Ayizan to show up occasionally by possessing someone. His presence will focus more on blessing the initiates. After that, you and the other initiates must remain secluded while doing certain activities that should not be revealed to anyone.

You must remain in seclusion for up to a week or seven days. Once you have completed that, expect to come out as a renewed, empowered, and strengthened version of yourself. You may even be reborn as someone new. It could be as a houngan, mambo, or a *hounsis.*

Before leaving your exact seclusion area, you must go through another ceremony called *brule kanzo.* Here, you will hold boiling cornmeal while being tested for your ability to handle fire. This activity is important, as it will serve as proof you are indeed strong.

When it is time to leave, you will be led on a procession once again while wearing white clothes and straw hats. You will be baptized as part of the community in the evening, followed by a party to honor your successful initiation and baptism.

Your successful completion of the seclusion period is your means of entry to the congregation and the entire community. The last stage of the whole initiation process will most likely involve you receiving a rattle. A Lwa may also possess you, as the new initiate, for the first time, which will mark the end of the initiation process.

## Should You Become an Initiate?

If you feel like being an initiate is your calling, then you should give it a go. Consider going through the entire initiation process so you can finally become a full-fledged voodooist. One thing to remember, though, is that not all people are fit for it. Not everyone finds the entire process desirable and is genuinely willing to handle the actual initiation's responsibilities.

Despite that, successful initiation comes with many rewards, though it also requires you to carry many responsibilities. Even if you are not born into this religion, you can still be a Voodooist if you want to be by approaching the right people in the community.

Communicate with a renowned and responsible houngan or mambo as much as possible. With their help, you can be initiated to be a Voodooist, hounsi, or even a houngan or mambo. Just get in touch with the most reputable community members who can invite you to the initiation after getting to know you and your potential.

Remember that being successfully accepted to the community somewhat resembles adoption or marriage if you decide to undergo the initiation. In other words, you will become a full-fledged member of a family. With that in mind, make sure you will be genuinely happy with your prospective new family. You need to open yourself up to them so they can learn more about you and accept you.

Patience is also important. Note that the entire process will be long, but it is all worth it. The best way to handle it is to ask questions regarding prospective teachers and initiators. Assess their reputation and credentials, too. Observe the way they work personally and the things they say whenever they communicate with others. If you plan to learn from a houngan or mambo, choose one with a verifiable and solid training and initiatory history.

Pick someone who is mature and has a lot of experience. You may have a challenging experience finding the right person to teach and train you during the initiation. Still, with patience and the constant seeking of guidance from your ancestors and spirits, you will ultimately find what you are looking for.

# Chapter 4: Voodoo Veves

Now, we will talk about the symbols or veves used in the Voodoo community. All Voodoo religion practitioners refer to the veves as drawings capable of representing or symbolizing the deities and the Lwas or spirits they worship.

Unlike other religions and traditions that use pictures and statues to symbolize their worshiped gods, the Voodoo community members are recognized for using veves or Voodoo symbols whenever their ceremonies occur. The Haitian Vodou tradition, for instance, is recognized for using various powders in tracing at least one esoteric sigil to represent every Lwa.

## A Closer Look at Veves

If you are not familiar with veves, the best way to describe them would be astral and spiritual scripts used to communicate with the Lwas or spirits. You can't consider them as stylized symbols that refer to complex iconographies. Instead, these veves are alphabets composing mystical phrases meant to summarize any metaphysical concepts, promoting ease in understanding them.

Besides the Voodoo symbols that characterize different Lwas, several other crucial elements appear in them. You must insert these additional crucial elements to provide more meaning or produce a more dynamic action to every accessible spiritual current.

As part of the Voodoo tradition, practitioners appeal to the Lwas or spirits and invite them to possess or ride human bodies. This is the only way to interact or communicate with them directly. With that, expect Voodoo rituals and ceremonies to involve a lot of dancing, chanting, music, and drumming. Besides all the mentioned practices, the participants must draw Voodoo symbols called veves.

These Voodoo symbols are important because they also appeal to certain Lwas, similar to how certain colors, chants, drumbeats, and objects do. You can't just draw any veve in a ritual or ceremony, though. Note you have to draw a symbol depending on the specific Lwa called upon in the ceremony.

Usually, drawing the symbols should be done on the ground. You have to use sand, cornmeal, or any other powdery substance to draw the symbol then obliterate it during the ceremony. As the veve symbolizes the actual figures of astral forces, it is crucial when appealing to any Lwa. During every ceremony, you can take advantage of the veve to reproduce the astral forces it represents, which will oblige the Lwas to come down to the Earth.

Another important fact about the veve symbols and designs is that each varies based on the local customs and the actual names of the Lwas. Some of these veves also share a few elements and similarities. One example is Damballah-Wedo, who is known as a serpent deity. Because of that, you will notice his veve often incorporating a couple of snakes.

As intricate symbols of Voodoo spirits or Lwas, it is necessary to use these veves in rituals and ceremonies. You can liken these Voodoo symbols to the sigils often used when doing ritual magic. Each veve is a material representation of a particular Lwa. Each symbol is a magic point. With that in mind, it is no longer surprising to see animal sacrifices and food offerings being placed on the drawn veve of the Lwa.

Each Voodoo symbol or veve is also made to graphically reproduce a Lwa's attributes and their ritual signs. Note that all Lwas have their own complex symbols or veves that the practitioners must trace on the ground before a ritual. This is done using a powdered eggshell or any other similar substance.

Anyone initiated to be part of the Voodoo tradition needs to be capable of drawing the veve correctly. The reason is this symbol will become even more powerful if you draw it using the right and accurate details.

# Most Important Veves in the Voodoo Community

With the numerous Lwas and spirits in the Voodoo religion, it is safe to say there are literally hundreds of veves you can use for any ritual or ceremony. However, out of these many veves, a few seem to be used more often, making them extremely important in all devotees and practitioners' lives. Some of the most important veves in this religion include:

## Veve of Aizan

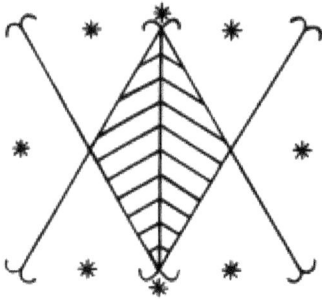

Aizan is recognized as the spirit or Lwa presiding over initiation rituals. She has such power because she, herself, is a mambo. The veve specifically used for this spirit is a couple of intertwined Vs. It refers to the primitive androgyne's V, which also features branches that have horns on their ends. You can see in the symbol a diamond in the center, which looks like a palm tree leaf with leaves.

The name of Ayizan means sacred earth. This name was also derived from the term, Aïzan, a Fon language, which means earthen mounds piling up the marketplace as a means of honoring primal ancestors. Her name was also derived from Azan, a relevant term, which means palm frond fringes that one can use in demarcating a sacred space. These origins of her name are why this Lwa holds a particular veve, with palm frond being her primary symbol.

Ayizan is also known for being the first or archetypal priestess or mambo, which is why she is often connected to priestly mystery and knowledge, including those related to the natural world and the initiation rites for any aspiring Voodoist.

As the Lwa of commerce and marketplace, you can call her to protect doors, entrances, barriers, gateways, public spaces, and markets. She can cleanse and purify a place and create a sacred space. The saint whom she is syncretized to in the Catholic Church is St. Claire.

Veve of Papa Legba

Papa Legba is probably the oldest and most vital Lwa or spirit in the Voodoo community. Many consider him the Lwa of entryways, doors, paths, gates, crossroads, trickery, and sorcery. He plays such an important role in the Voodoo community in the sense that other spirits or Lwas will not get to the Earth without his permission.

As he holds the keys for both humans and Lwas to interact, you can see him being identified with the famous Catholic saint, St. Peter. Just like St. Peter, Papa Legba also acts as a strong foundation for the religion. Papa Legba's veve or Voodoo symbol features a cross with equal sides. This makes him strongly connected to the cross, which is why many Voodooists perceive Papa Legba as the community's Christ.

Since he is also the master of crossroads, you can see Papa Legba governing sorcery. He is even considered the greatest magician ever introduced. Papa Legba is also considered by the Voodoo community as the sun, an element worshipped by practitioners as a force that gives life. Perceived as the sun, Papa Legba also represents the East and the orient, the specific place where it is possible to control magic and create life.

This transformed him into the God of creation. The cardinal point you can see in the magical cross in his symbol is the East. This makes it crucial for him to be greeted first whenever he welcomes spirits or

Lwas. It will be easier for him to open the doors, allowing other spirits to enter.

As the master of highways and guardian of crossroads, you can also see Papa Legba having crossroads as part of his symbolisms. These crossroads represent the union of vertical and horizontal astral forces, making it possible for Papa Legba to control the spirit or the God's astral-causal magic.

Drawings representing Papa Legba also perceive him as an old man. Voodooists relate him to water bearers. The reason is that he also has full control of the Earth's fluid, particularly circulation and blood. Moreover, he represents bones, bone marrow, and vertebrae. You can see these items being symbolized by a central post known for being the peristyle's backbone.

### Veve of Agwe

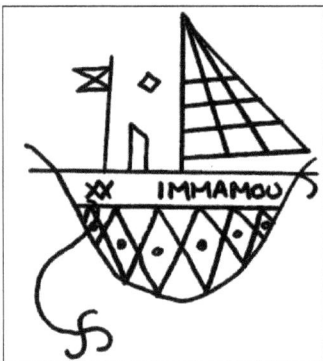

Agwe, the spirit ruling the fish, aquatic plants, and the sea, is the patron Lwa of all the sailors and fishermen in the Voodoo community, particularly those in Haiti. Many invoke him using the names tadpole of the pond and seashell. Under Agwe's influence, it is possible to witness many flora and fauna in the sea. You can also find many boats sailing in the sea because of his influence, which is why a boat is part of his veve or Voodoo symbol.

The veve of Agwe features brightly painted boats. These boats could also be shells or oars. There are also instances when small metal fish are used in place of the boat symbol. It is crucial to note that the process of serving Agwe differs from when calling other spirits or Lwas. The reason is that Agwe, himself, can also be seen in the sea.

With that in mind, you can see many Voodooists using actual shells, besides the Voodoo symbol they draw for him when summoning or invoking him, during celebrations or rituals. You must welcome him with a towel and wet sponge whenever you see him coming out of the water because of the heat.

To worship or call upon him, it is often necessary to prepare a boat containing all the foods he favors (including savory and exotic foods), and other things he likes, including champagne, naval rum, toy ships, and gunfire. The siren of the sea, La Sirene, is known for being the female counterpart of Agwe. He is also the counterpart of St. Ulrich in the Roman Catholic religion.

### Veve of Damballah-Vedo

Another veve that all members of the Voodoo community consider as extremely important is that of Damballah-Vedo. As the Lwa of snakes, serpents, rain, life, and water, you can see his Voodoo symbol or veve appearing like two prominent serpents. This veve reflects the fact that most Voodooists depict him as a snake or serpent.

He has a strong connection with the ancestors. Damballah-Vedo is also one of the wisest and oldest Lwas, together with his partner in creation, Ayida-Wedo. The fact that the entire creative process has to be shared by a man and woman is why his veve comes with two snakes or serpents instead of just one.

The important role played by Damballah-Vedo in the Voodoo community can never be underestimated. He is strongly linked to the process of creation, making him a prominent figure. Besides that, Damballah-Vedo is also recognized for his ability to bring harmony and peace.

### Veve of Baron Samedi

Baron Samedi, the head of the Ghede family representing all dead and living souls, also has his own veve or Voodoo symbol. This symbol mainly has a cross, though this cross does not symbolize the one used by Christians or the Roman Catholics. What it symbolizes, instead, is a crossroad.

The reason could be that you can usually find Baron Samedi at the crossroads, specifically between the worlds of those already dead and the living. Part of his routine is digging graves for the dead and greeting their souls after burial. He will then lead these dead souls to the underworld.

You can also find two interlocking V's drawn vertically in the veve of Baron Samedi. These figures symbolize the union of two sexes considered as the major components of the primitive androgyne. The veve also features three degrees or steps, the one where the cross stands, and each step represents the level of initiation. The first step is a symbol of ordinary life, so you can see it being decorated by phalluses and working instruments.

The second step symbolizes the movement that the *acon* (a sacred rattle that a priest uses) traces in the air. The highest step or degree represents the secret held by the best among those who became priests. The one who holds this secret is also known for being gifted with double vision. Overall, this veve is so powerful that it illustrates the strong connection between death and the afterlife.

**Veve of Ougon**

Part of the Rada family is the spirit (Lwa) known as Ougon. The primary Voodoo symbols used for this Lwa include iron, palm frond, and a dog. These symbols or veves represent the significant role played by Ougon in terms of mediation, function, and transformation. The fact that iron is this spirit's main emblem or symbol is also why most ceremonies and altars dedicated to him use and display objects made of iron.

This means that aside from drawing the veve, you may also summon him by wearing chains with iron implements. Festivals honoring Ougon also usually display guns, knives, wrenches, scissors, blacksmith implements, and any other implements based on iron that most use in daily life. The Voodoo symbol of Ougon is also proof he is a deity (orisha) and spirit (Lwa) capable of presiding over things like iron, war, politics, and hunting.

Ougon is also recognized in the community as the god of intelligence, political power, pioneering, medicine, and justice. These can be connected to the symbol of the exact tool capable of advancing humans' mastery over the surrounding environment. In Africa, you can see Ougon being worshiped by many blacksmiths, with most originating from Yoruba. Ougon also favors alcohol and women.

### Veve of Gran Bwa

Another Lwa who plays a huge role in the Voodoo community is Gran Bwa. A part of the Petro family, Gran Bwa strongly connects with magic, secrets, and healing. He can conceal specific items from the eyes of those who are not initiated in this religion. Many summon him during initiation ceremonies.

He is considered the master of Vilokan's forests because he is the reason behind his symbol or veve, which you can see as strongly linked to plants and trees. The name given to him, Gran Bwa, also means big tree, which is why his symbol also somewhat signifies this connection.

Aside from his strong connection with trees and plants, Gran Bwa also represents the practices linked to them, including herbalism. This spirit is also recognized as the master of the wilderness, so his personality includes unpredictability and wildness. Despite that, he also shows many great qualities, including being a fairly approachable and loving Lwa.

One specific object that Gran Bwa considers sacred is silk cotton or the mapou tree. This tree is a native of Haiti, which connects the spiritual and material worlds. You can often see mapou being represented by a central pole in Voodoo temples' courtyards. Gran Bwa also gained the recognition of being a protector and guardian of ancestors who travel from one world to the next all the time.

### Veve of Erzulie Freda

Erzulie Freda is also a prominent Lwa in the Voodoo community, so her veve is popular. As the goddess of beauty and love, it is no longer surprising to see her veve coming with a squared heart at the center. This makes her Voodoo symbol more representative of romantic love, luxury, and sweetness. You can summon her whenever you feel like it is time to add more luxury and love to your life.

Each square and inner point found in this veve or symbol also symbolizes a force ready to explode. You can also see a voodoo star on top of it and two rising moons. You can find the quintessential sun spirit, which is a staff of Papa Legba. This indicates that uniting feminine and masculine principles is what results in love. It fuses and unites fire and water together.

Another thing you will notice in the veve of Erzulie Freda is the large loops on its sides. This represents balance, which means that there should be no prevailing principle. You can also see an inverted ram's horns in the veve, which signifies possession.

This could mean the desire of Erzulie Freda to get more from those who worship and follow her. Despite her wealth, she still finds the world disappointing and constantly reminds everyone that material things should not be the only wealth you can attain.

# How to Draw Voodoo Symbols (Veves)

Now that you know some of the most commonly used veves or symbols in Voodoo, it is time to know more about how you can make one yourself. Note that veves serve as powerful tools you can use to connect with a higher energy and Voodoo magic, spirits, and deities.

You need to draw the veves on the ground using any powdery substance like sand and cornmeal. You then have to obliterate them during ceremonies and rituals. You have to trace the drawings manually on the ground before the start of a ritual or ceremony.

Besides sand and cornmeal, you can also use coffee powder, white flour, herbs, and brick powder for the purpose. Your choice will greatly depend on the specific division and mystery you intend to evoke. To scatter the powder, slide it between your thumb and middle and index fingers. Use the fingers on your right hand, so you can attain regular traces.

After tracing the veve, you have to spray it with a suitable libation. Put a candle at the center, then activate it by ringing either a maraca or bell. While doing so, recite prayers and invocations to the mystery of the multiple Lwas you intend to call, summon, or invoke.

If you perform a Voodoo service as a means of feeding a few Lwas simultaneously, then incorporate all their ritual emblems in the veve when drawing it. Make sure that all Lwas are part of your drawn symbol. This may cause the final symbol or veve to be complex while also covering a huge part of the peristyle.

It is possible to make the veve into a painting, screen-print, patchwork, banner, artwork, and wall hanging. However, take note it would be much better to handcraft or draw it yourself. Remember that it will become more powerful and effective in summoning Lwas and manifesting your heart's desires if you draw it manually.

When drawing the veve, it would also be much better to use both your hands. By doing that, the entire process will surely symbolize the pathways one has to take to get into the worlds of the invisible and visible. In most cases, this pathway is around the Poteau mitan or center pole. This spot forms a new conduit where the divine can easily travel.

Make sure that you also draw the symbol correctly. It is the key to summoning the correct Lwa. If you draw it incorrectly, then it will only lead to summoning shadows or malevolent spirits. An incorrectly drawn veve may also result in summoning the wrong Lwa, someone for whom the ritual or ceremony was not made.

Do not forget to bless the completed drawing of the veve with sacred waters, too. You can also use alcohol or rum for this purpose. Another important part of the ritual involves drawing a veve to summon a Lwa is dancing. It is crucial for those who participate in the ritual or ceremony to dance on the drawn veves barefoot.

This is essential to assist divine energies to penetrate their bodies, allowing spiritual possession to take place. It also contributes to the veve setting the stage for communicating and communing with the divine.

## Using Veves in Talismans or Flags

Most of those who are already familiar with using talismans fully know how useful the symbols integrated into them are –especially when it comes to protecting themselves from evil and attracting fortune, or whatever their intention is. When planning to use these talismans, though, remember that the symbols required differ based on their origin.

If you are from the Voodoo community, then the symbols you have to integrate into the talismans should be the corresponding symbols in the religion, known as veves. These talismans include amulets, trinkets, jewelry pieces, or even a small flag you can use to keep yourself protected or draw positive things to you, like prosperity, money, love, and health.

Being sacred tools, you need to charge them using the waxing moon's power. They serve as magical tools capable of generating positive energies that can attract whatever you desire. To use veves in talismans, follow these basic steps:

• **Decide On the Reason You Need the Talisman** – Once you know your intention, conduct research on the seals, planets, and the specific spirits or Lwas linked to the things you intend to attract.

• **Collect Important and Useful Items, Like Bones, Stones, Herbs, and Crystals** – Ensure you pick those with a strong connection to your talisman's intended purpose. Your goal is to seek the help of the intended spirit to determine what you think is right and appropriate.

• **Draw the Veve or Voodoo Symbol** – This is necessary to enchant your talisman. Ensure that you also write a message, which states the specific thing you want your talisman to do. Remove all vowels from the message. Remove every third letter of the words, then rearrange the remaining ones until an abstract image is formed, which differs from the original statement. After that, you can draw the veve or symbol in a cloth bag.

• **Build Your Ritual Space** – Ensure it contains everything needed for the ritual or ceremony. Among the things, you may need frankincense or sandalwood incense and white candles. These are often good tools you can use to set up your ritual space and make it as sacred as possible.

- **Choose to Do the Ritual When You Can Focus Intently** – Do it privately and when you are alone. If possible, pick a planetary hour or day, which corresponds to your talisman's main purpose.

- **Encircle Yourself With Lighted Candles** – Summon the gods and spirits you believe in when doing so. Also dedicate a few minutes to meditation. Ensure that you focus intently on the veve or symbol. Meditate based on your heart's desires. Stay away from all forms of distraction and communicate or interact with the related spirits.

- **Once Done, Hold the Talisman** – Recite your intentions or wishes when doing so.

During the last step, visualize the answers that your summoned Lwa or spirit may give you. Do it while the talisman continues to warm up with your body's heat. Feel the excitement of your intentions coming to life. Allow the energy to flow not only to your hands but also to the talisman.

Observe the talisman. Once you feel like it completely absorbed all the energy, you can use a gesture to seal it off. For instance, if you put the items inside a bag, you can seal them off by kissing them. Then feel joy once you notice your desire happening.

To use the talisman, you can wear it or put it in your room. Another way to use it is to put it inside a pouch and carry or wear it. Fortunately, you can also put it in a box and place it on your altar whenever you do not feel the need to wear it.

## Should You Use Veve Tattoos?

Many people now decide to put tattoos of Voodoo symbols or veves on their bodies. This is a mistake, and you should avoid doing it at all costs. Remember that the veve is a Voodoo symbol primarily meant to be drawn on a floor or a sacred object during a ritual.

Each of these veves is linked to a specific spirit. It is drawn during a ceremony as a means of capturing the attention of a Lwa. That it is a sacred symbol to the Voodoo community makes it quite unpleasant to put it on your body. It should be used at the appropriate time and place. Putting it on your body in the form of a tattoo may invite unwanted effects and issues as it may lead to inviting negative energies and the wrong spirits.

# Chapter 5: Build Your Voodoo Shrine

If you are serious about becoming a Voodoo practitioner and devotee, you have to learn how to build your own voodoo altar or shrine. It should be dedicated to the ancestor or Lwa you favor and want to summon all the time. It may be a daunting task, especially for those who are still beginners in this religion, but once you have everything ready, you can learn the basics and eventually master how to prepare and build your Voodoo shrine.

## Types of Altars

The first step you have to take when building your Voodoo shrine or altar is to determine its exact purpose. This will show you the specific type of shrine or altar you have to build. It will guide you to determine the tools and objects you need and the requirements you have to adhere to, especially regarding the positioning and placement of the sacred items.

Here are the different types of altar or shrine you can build:

- **Ancestor Altar** - You can build this one if your goal is to connect with your ancestors. You will be putting pictures of your departed loved ones on the altar. You may also include some of their personal items, particularly those they love, to serve as their reminders. It is also advisable to put a plate and cup for food and drink offerings.

- **Deity Altar** - As the name suggests, this altar is meant to worship Lwas, spirits, and deities. You can make this altar a shared space but make sure that the specific spirits and deities you intend to summon permit it. For this altar to work, dedicate a space to leave your offerings. There should also be a space where you can light candles and incense and offer items that the spirit or deity favors. Sometimes, the altar holds idols as a means of standing in for the Lwas or spirits you intend to worship or honor in that space.

- **Nature Altar** - You can also dedicate a space designed to honor nature. In most cases, you can see these altars being filled with things representing the natural elements - among which are seashells and stones. Remember that the nature altar can't be used as a sacred space for your offerings.

- **Temporary Altar** - You can create this type of altar for certain events, like a festival meant to worship or honor a certain Lwa or deity. You can also use it whenever you need to do a certain magical rite. It is meant for rituals and holidays. That it is temporary means you can dismantle it right after the event.

The specific purpose you intend your altar to perform should be the deciding factor on the type you have to choose.

# Finding the Appropriate Space

After deciding on the type of altar or shrine to build, the next thing you should do is to look for the right space where you can set it up. You need enough space so you can comfortably perform the ritual. Some things you can use as your altar or shrine would be:

• **A Small Table** – You may want to use your coffee or end table for your altar. One advantage is that you can easily move it, plus it provides a clean and flat surface capable of holding various things. You can also thrift it conveniently. Just make sure you spend time cleaning the table before using it.

• **The Top of Your Dresser** – If you have an unused dresser at home, then you can use the top for your sacred altar or shrine. It is a great idea, especially if you have kids and pets at home since they can't easily reach it. Since it is a dresser, you can put it in a place where people can see right away and interact or communicate every day. It may not be a suitable choice for you, though, if you are uncomfortable setting up your altar or shrine in your own room.

• **Cabinet** – You can also use any cabinet you can find at home. It provides adequate space, plus it comes with multiple levels, giving you the chance to pick a level for a specific purpose. If you have only a small space, then you can set aside a bit of space from a desk, bookshelf, or dresser in your home.

However, ensure that even if you're sharing a particular space, avoid allowing items that are not supposed to be in the altar to take the space dedicated for it.

Consider and prioritize privacy, too. Despite having a full closet to accommodate a huge setup for your altar, it will be hard to do your rituals or ceremonies if you display it out in the open. You can put a tiny altar in a closet, which you can close-at any time.

Those are just a few examples of items of spaces that you can set aside for your altar or shrine. Remember that your choice serves as an external representation of inner mysteries. It tangibly shows what may happen in your spirits and hearts. This means you have to choose the most suitable space wisely.

Also, the shrine or altar you have built is the key for you to reflect, honor, remember, and heal from grief – anytime you want. It works as your private space – one that lets you reflect, grieve, meditate, honor, remember, and engage in personal rituals with anyone who has departed.

You can also use a small and portable shrine – one you can conveniently carry anywhere you want. It could be an extremely small one, like a matchbook, which can easily fit your pocket. You can also use a bigger one but that you can easily slip into your briefcase or purse.

By choosing a shrine you can carry anywhere, it will be easy for you to maintain the connection you have established with your loved one – even those who have died. It also gives you a sacred space you can use to remember someone or perform a personal ritual regardless of where you are.

# What Do You Need for Your Voodoo Altar/Shrine?

Once you already have a space for your altar or shrine, it is time to gather the things necessary for you to make it work for your Voodoo rituals. You may want to put a few things on the altar, such as your magical tools. However, remember that the ultimate goal should be to make the altar as functional as possible. With that in mind, you have to set it up with items that will let you attain your goals.

Some things that include the altar are:

• *Symbols of four classical elements* – These elements are the earth, air, fire, and water. It is crucial to align these elements with the four corresponding cardinal directions. Here, you have to use a bowl containing sand or earth in your altar's north aspect to represent the earth, incense in the east to represent air, water in the west, and charcoal or candle in the south to symbolize fire.

• *Candles* – Your altar should also have candles. It could be a god candle or goddess candle, depending on what your ritual or spell requires. It would also be best to choose different colors for the candles. You may also use candles that represent the four directions. Just ensure that you also have a match or lighter so you can easily light them.

• *Wand* – You may also want to put a wand on your altar. This wand is often helpful in directing energy. Note that the specific manner through which you will be laying this wand and the exact spot where you will be putting it on the altar will greatly depend on what you intend to do, but wise advice is to put it close to or on the altar.

• *Athame* – You can also put an athame on your altar. It refers to a blunt and double-edged blade used in channeling energy. It often has a black handle and blunt blade, which helps prevent accidents during ceremonies and rituals. One thing you should remember about an athame is to prevent yourself from using it for physical cutting. What you have to do, instead, is use it for cutting energy symbolically. With the athame in your altar, you can guide energy every time you do your rituals or ceremonies.

• *An item that makes your shrine or altar unique from its surrounding*s – If you set up the altar in a different spot, use a table cover or cloth. It should indicate that the entire space is dedicated to the Voodoo altar or shrine.

If you set it up in a shared space, like the top of your dresser or your work desk, then look for an item that will instantly send a warning that a particular space is only meant for the altar. By doing that, you can maintain the orderliness and cleanliness of that particular spot. It can also prevent you from placing other things that are not supposed to be on the altar.

One thing you can do is to create a small crate or box. It should serve as the shrine. You may also set it up as a tray where you can keep important things on.

• *A spot where you can put anything you want to offer to the Lwa or ancestor* – It could be a small dish or tray. Dedicate it to the offerings so you can easily monitor what you have left in there during the ritual.

• *A clear space where you can put temporary items* – There should be a clear space dedicated for some temporary items you need. It is advisable to put divinatory tools on your altar, so you can bless or charge them right away. Some examples would be certain icons designed to represent specific issues you feel require help. By dedicating a clear space for such a purpose, you can prevent the order of your altar from being untidy.

• *A personal item so valuable and meaningful to you* – You may want to put such things if you want your altar to have some personal effects. By putting something meaningful to you on your altar, you can easily create a channel between the actual practice and you. You may add a painting, idol, a specific incense, or anything that is personal to you and meets your specific needs.

Place any other item you think you need and have the available space for. You may also want to put any components of the spell you need, like ale and cakes. If you plan to use your altar to celebrate a particular event or holiday that specifically points to the Lwa you intend to summon, decorate your altar based on that, too. Ensure that the altar has everything you need to do your rituals effectively.

# Building Your Altar

Once you have chosen the space, the things you need, and the actual altar you will be using, it is time for you to set it up. It is crucial to note that you can create the altar either for a public or private space. The only things you should never forget incorporating into this space are respect and sincerity. Ensure that you also build your altar based on these tips:

• Clean the surface first using a spiritual solution, such as rose water or Florida water. Wipe it dry, then pray aloud to express your desire to make the space and specific surface intended for the altar holy.

• If you are using a table constructed from wooden material, you can bless it using oil, such as ancestor or Van oil. After that, look for a cloth you can use to cover the altar. It is preferable to use white, but you can also be more creative in your cloth choice. Try avoiding synthetic materials and dark colors, though. It would be best to go for cotton then use it to cover the altar.

• Make sure to put beautiful and meaningful objects on the altar. They can be Voodoo dolls, statues, talismans, roots, stones, or flowers. Pick things that have special meaning or those that inspire you. The altar should also contain incense, candles, anointing oils, or perfumes.

• Put water on the altar. Another tip for setting up the perfect Voodoo altar or shrine is to regularly put water on it. It can contribute a lot to gaining more clarity in life. Do not forget to change the water frequently.

• Identify the exact purpose of the altar. You can make it to honor the dead or living, particularly those who have inspired you. If so, then ensure that you put pictures of them on the altar, too.

• Meditate before the shrine or altar you have built every day. This should serve as your daily ritual. When meditating, concentrate on the positive changes you intend to make happen in your life and in the lives of your family members, loved ones, and the entire Voodoo community.

In most cases, all Voodoo devotees, even priests, make it a point to build a small altar designed for a certain Lwa in their households. They use these altars or shrines as focal points for their meditation and prayer. It is at this altar or shrine that they perform private devotionals. This private home altar specifically designated for a Lwa is called an *ogantwa.*

This ogantwa holds many items found in hounfo's *badji* (temple room), such as lithographs or exact representations of the spirit or Lwa, satin scarves made of different colors, thunderstones, and dolls. You may also have to put a kind of perpetual lamp here. You can also make a basic ogantwa using a shelf or table or a cabinet. Each is dedicated to a certain Lwa.

To make this ogantwa work for your chosen Lwa, put an image of a saint or spirit. An example is St. Claire, who is a spirit capable of bringing about illumination and clarity. Other examples of images you can use are those of the Holy Virgin, Danbala (St. Patrick), Papa Legba, Papa Ogou (St. George, and Mater Dolorosa (Ezili Freda).

Just like water being important for an altar designed for general or multiple purposes, you also need a bowl or glass of fresh water placed on the ogantwa for it to work. As a devotee, you may need to put a bell or rattle there so you can easily call the spirits. Other items you should put in your shrine are a glass bowl designed for lamp making, olive oil, cotton wicks, white taper candles, and a small brazier you can use for the incense.

Baptize the ogantwa, too. This is the key to cleansing and blessing it before each use. Usually, you will be asked to burn frankincense then recite three prayers, like Our Father or Hail Mary, for a certain period. After that, sprinkle your ogantwa with holy water taken from Catholic churches. This should be enough to baptize the ogantwa. Once done, you can start using it to act as your focal point for meditation and prayer.

# Chapter 6: How to Make a Gris-Gris Bag

A gris-gris bag is one of the most popular items used by Voodooists. It is extremely popular in the Voodoo community for many good reasons. The origin of this bag can be traced back to West Africa. It started due to the influences made by Muslim scholars, mystics, and healers. After that, the use of this bag got absorbed by the cultures in Africa. It contributed its shaping and transformation based on the local customs and beliefs in the country.

The original gris-gris contained a folded paper with a Quran inscription. You can see this inscription being written using special ink. You may also find significant numbers, symbols, and words on the piece of paper. It was tied and folded using a string then stored in a leather-made pouch. This way, one could easily put it on his body or affix it to a certain, meaningful location.

Let's dive deeper into what a gris-gris bag is and how to create one through this article.

# Gris-Gris Bag Defined

A gris-gris bag refers to a powerful charm bag constructed from chamois or red flannel. Note that such a trait is unchangeable. This means that the bag's color, the chamois or red flannel, should remain fixed. If the gris-gris bag you intend to use makes calls for a certain color, put one piece of such material inside.

For example, if the bag needs an orange color, look for a fabric piece in that shade. Just cut a small piece from this material, then put it inside the bag. It should be enough to handle the required color correspondence. You can make this bag in a similar way you create a sachet or mojo bag. The only thing that distinguishes it from the others is that it needs to be a certain color.

In Voodoo, the gris-gris bag aims to offer protection from evil. Many Voodooists also believe that it is effective in bringing luck. Some West African countries also use it as a birth control technique. It comes in the form of a small bag made of cloth. Voodooists inscribe it with verses derived from their African ancestors. This inscription often comes with a ritual number of tiny objects. They then wear it on almost all occasions.

You can wear the gris-gris bag in any part of your body. It could be on your limbs, waist, or neck. However, remember that the exact spot where you will be wearing it is often linked to the bag's purpose. You may wear it for health, love, social harmony, or protection, and each specific purpose requires a different placement.

# Ingredients for Your Gris-Gris Bag

The gris-gris bag will always play a major part in the Voodoo tradition. As a matter of fact, it is the predecessor of Voodoo dolls. You can still see the gris-gris bag being used today, particularly in the New Orleans tradition, to gain protection from evil, attracting love, and manifesting luck, career growth, and money.

This bag is around 5 x 8 cm and made from thin leather, suede, or flannel by tradition. It is also necessary to fill the bag with specific items and materials, including dried herbs, talismans, amulets, coins, bones, and crushed minerals. Every item or element placed in the bag has a specific symbolism and purpose.

# Plants and Herbs

Plants and herbs are among the most commonly used fillers in Voodoo's gris-gris bags. Each has a distinctive symbolism and quality you have to consider during the preparation. Some examples are:

- Alfalfa – to attain luck in business and gambling. It is also perfect when planning to protect yourself from bankruptcy and other financial or money issues.

- Aloe Vera – to protect from negative forces and influences

- Anise – to attain spiritual protection from bad luck. It also boosts your physical abilities and brings luck and fortune.

- Bay leaf – to gain spiritual protection, success, and good health. You can also use it for your gris-gris bag to attain mental clarity, banish evil spirits, strengthen wisdom, and emerge as a victor over your enemies.

- Black pepper – to prevent unwanted visits

- Catnip – to attract love. Women can also use it to attract the male.

- Dandelion – to fulfill your desires

- Eucalyptus – to protect you from bad luck and get rid of unwanted and bad habits

- Licorice – to gain control or dominance over someone

- Parsley – to attract love and encourage fertility

- Rosemary – to dismiss evil spirits and promote the well-being of the entire family

- Sage – to attain purification, genuine happiness, and wisdom

- Sweet pepper – to gain luck, especially in business and when gambling. It also helps in removing stress.

- Thyme – to achieve tranquility and peace, get rid of nightmares, and preserve wealth

- Yarrow – to gain courage

# Stones and Minerals

You can also fill your gris-gris bag with stones and minerals. For you to use them effectively, you have to crush them to dust first. After that, combine the crushed stones and minerals with dried herbs. You can use them for many things, including success, health, spiritual protection, and love. Here are a few of those that you can use:

- Agate – You can use the white agate if you want to attain good health and the dark-colored ones if you want to be lucky whenever you gamble.

- Amber – for luck and love

- Amethyst – for spiritual protection and better health

- Colorless quartz – for better health, peace, happiness, and protection

- Flint – for better health and protection against all forms of hazards

- Gold – to gain money, wealth, and success

- Jasper – to obtain protection from a wide range of negativities and unwanted results

- Moonstone – for protection against the dangers associated with love

- Topaz – for health and spiritual protection

- Turquoise – for health and protection against negative results

# Other Materials and Objects

Besides the herbs, stones, and minerals, you can also fill up your gris-gris bag with various materials and objects holding various meanings. Among the most commonly used ones are:

- Nail – to gain protection from negative results

- Dollar sign illustration – to attain luck when gambling

- Keys – to attract love

- A piece of red brick – to attract success and money and gain household protection

- Magnet – to manifest fortune and attract gifts. You can also use it to get the attention of people.

- Ammonia – to promote cleansing and gain protection from harsh effects

- Sugar – to attract love and success in a romantic relationship. It is also meant to manifest money or profit into a business.

- Salt – to promote spiritual cleansing and get rid of bad luck

- Lodestones – It is advisable to use the lodestones in pairs to attract positive forces and repelling the negative ones.

- Cross – to represent your faith and attain blessing and spiritual protection

- Dice – to gain more luck whenever you take on a game of chance or gamble

- Coins – to attract prosperity and money

- Personal items, like hair, photos, or nail clippings – to connect the amulet's energy to a certain person

- A piece of feather or colored cloth – to increase the color correspondences of the amulet

• Written talisman on a parchment – to increase the planetary influences of the amulet or improve its intent even further

• A saint's card or medal – Add the suitable patron saint medal to further strengthen your intent. It is also helpful to invoke the saint or spirit's aid.

• Magical powder and oil – You may also add magical powders and oils to strengthen the amulet's intent.

# The Actual Making of the Gris-Gris Bag

Making the gris-gris bag is not that complicated, provided you gather all the necessary things. You can use any of the special herbs, stones, and objects stated in this chapter to make it work. You may also want to fill it up with roots, personal effects, crystals, European sigils and seals, and other lucky charms. Aside from all those possible fillers, you can also add other colors into it based on magical symbolism.

To know how many items you should put in the bag, then the answer would be an odd number that is not less than three and not over thirteen. It is also crucial to bless the items while putting them inside the bag. Use holy water or anointing oil to dress up the entire bag, too.

After that, a smudge in any kind of incense. Speak some words of power to it, then breathe upon it. Those are effective rituals capable of activating the power of gris-gris. If you plan to practice New Orleans Voodoo, remember that the gris-gris bag they create is usually concealed from public view. You also have to prepare it ritually on an altar then consecrate it to the four classic elements – fire, air, water, and earth.

The actual creation of the gris-gris bag also requires you to remember a few points and rules, among which the following are worthy of note:

• Color symbolism will always play a significant role in creating the bag – Pick a color specifically designed for your needs.

- Fill the bag with items that can specifically meet your desired purpose.

- Dress up the bag with a kind of liquid. It could be holy water or anointing oil.

- Be extra cautious of the things you say when creating the bag. Remember that the words that come out of your mouth can create strong energy, becoming a major component of the gris-gris bag.

- Smudge or smoke with incense every ingredient you intend to put inside the bag – Do the same to the final bag, too.

- Place or sew into the bag a written petition – This petition needs to be written using a magical alphabet. Alternatively, you can draw a magical seal or sigil on parchment paper using magical ink. Place it inside or sew it into the bag. You may also want to add some magic squares and talismans to the bag.

- Speak powerful words when creating the bag – This is crucial in the activation of only divine energy.

- Give life to your gris-gris bag by breathing upon it.

- Respect and match each filler ingredient's symbolism to a certain gris-gris bag.

- Lubricate the bag's surface using an oil connected to your purpose.

- Use incense or candle smoke to fumigate the bag before each use.

Just remember those tips when making your own gris-gris bag. One final note to consider is to ensure that you already visualize your end goal. Determine what you genuinely intend to achieve from creating this bag. After that, constantly think about the manner through which it will come true.

Once you have completed your gris-gris bag, put it or hang it in an open and prominent place - one you can see easily while letting you concentrate on it in private. That way, it will always remind you of your wish. To use it in the right way, say your own heartfelt prayer. Just hold it in your palms with your two hands close together, then bring it up to your mouth. After that, activate the bag using your breath by blowing into it.

Another thing to remember is to recharge it. You can do so by soaking it in whiskey every Friday. To use it to prevent evil from getting inside your home, then hang the bag over your doorway. You may also want to use a leather cord so you can wear the bag around your neck.

Alternatively, you can take it with you anywhere by putting it in your pocket. Just put it at the right spot - the right pocket if you are a man and the left pocket if you are a woman.

## Can You Make Gris-Gris Dolls?

Yes, you can make your own gris-gris doll. The only thing you have to do is to prepare a black fabric and make a doll from it. It should be small enough. Then fill the doll with symbolic things, like salt, saffron, powdered dog manure, crumpled newspaper taken from an obituary, gunpowder, and graveyard dirt.

Once you have this gris-gris doll, you can use it for your intended purpose. Note there are several ways for you to use and work with these Voodoo dolls that will be explained in the next chapter.

# Chapter 7: Working With Dolls

Voodoo dolls tend to spark fear from anyone unfamiliar with what they truly are. Hearing about and seeing these dolls will most likely invoke bloodthirsty and violent scenarios, particularly those you have watched in films or read in books.

The most common belief about Voodoo dolls is that they are made by anyone who wants to gain revenge or has a grudge against their enemy. You will notice some pins that the one who made it uses to thrust into the doll. The maker will then curse his target with pain, death, or any other form of misfortune.

Now the question is, is this really what Voodoo dolls are all about?

## What Are Voodoo Dolls?

A voodoo doll is a small human effigy constructed from a couple of sticks tied together to form a cross shape and create a body with both arms sticking out. You can then see this shape is covered by a triangular cloth in bright colors. There are also several cases when it uses Spanish moss to fill it out and maintain the form of the body. It has a head made of wood or black cloth.

This doll comes with rudimentary facial features, including a mouth, a pair of eyes, and a nose. Those who constantly make Voodoo dolls also decorate them using sequins and feathers. In most cases, there will be pins to insert into the doll for any intention or purpose.

The voodoo doll also comes in various forms – one of which is the gris-gris doll briefly mentioned in the previous chapter. You can also see the practice of using it in many magical traditions based on different cultures worldwide.

Generally, you can see this figure being used in Haiti's Vodou religion. It is used as a major part of the tradition brought over from Western Africa with tiny effigies called a *bocio* or fetish they incorporated to perform rituals. When the slaves from Africa were forced to move to the new world, the *caldoches* brought their tradition of using this doll with them.

African shamans used this doll to interact or communicate with the Lwa and their dead ancestors to gain guidance. Eventually, they noticed how reliable this tool was for that purpose. It is the reason you can still see this Voodoo doll being used for essential rituals.

The general use of this doll, though, is to heal. Contrary to what others believe, it does not primarily aim to cause harm to people. Some also use it to maintain an open line of communication to the world of the departed. This means they use it to contact their recently departed loved ones.

Eventually, though, using voodoo dolls became more expansive, especially after the mish-mash of Catholicism, Voodoo, Native American healing arts, and European folk magic. It prompted the use of this doll in various ways, like the one that involves colored pins.

Besides that, the voodoo doll is also said to promote love, protection, success, and healing, among many others. While the Voodoo religion is a mystery to some, it still carries tools designed to promote change, like the voodoo dolls.

# Ideal Materials for Your Voodoo Doll

Are you interested in making your own Voodoo doll? Then take note there are several materials you can use for this purpose. Remember that you may create your desired doll based on how you want it. Just make sure that it will have a direct spiritual and materialistic connection to the one you intend to reach out to through it.

You can make your own Voodoo doll from any material you can get hold of – among which are:

• **Clay** – The voodoo dolls used in the Louisiana/New Orleans tradition were traditionally created from blue clay taken from the burrows of crayfish. It is also possible for you to use any kind of clay when creating yours.

You just have to make sure that once you finish creating your Voodoo doll made of clay, you maintain the hollow void inside of it. This is the specific spot where you can put certain materials that belong to or symbolize your subject. One example is an herb. Once you have formed the doll, you can paint and apply to it any magical symbol.

• **Wax** – You can also use wax for your Voodoo doll project. Some consider this material as almost perfect in all aspects. One advantage of it is its flexibility. It also works great as it can retain its original form and shape. It means it is long-lasting.

Many of those who make Voodoo dolls prefer wax because they can easily portray the human form. It is also easy to carve magic symbols on this material. You can attach someone's hair to it, making it more effective in building a connection.

• **Spanish Moss** – This material is a classic for the New Orleans tradition. What is great about Spanish moss is that it works impressively as stuffing or fillers for furniture and pillows, among many other things. It is the main reason this material is famous in Southern US. You can also see many Louisiana sorcerers using it successfully. One version of the Voodoo doll made out of this plant is the traditional type with no legs.

• **Cloth** – You can also make your own Voodoo doll made of cloth. One example is a rag doll constructed out of a couple of strips of material. You have only to embroider them into two identical forms on both sides of the doll. This can leave a hole, which will let you fill the doll with magical items, like common moss and herbs.

• **Wood** – If you want a more primitive style, you can create your Voodoo doll from wood. Before using this material, one thing to remember is that it can only depict the form of humans with fewer details. The reason is that it can work as a portrayal in a more generalized manner.

Sometimes, you can carve the doll in just one wooden piece. You need to be extremely accurate and skillful when doing so. A simple version would be a thick tree branch that uses moss as a covering. You can then trim it with a cloth and carve a face to help the figure appear more realistic.

• **Paper** – It is also possible for you to create your own version of the Voodoo doll from paper. One way to use paper to create the voodoo doll is to turn the material into a pulp first. Soak the pulped paper and combine it with an adhesive component. After that, you can use the same methods as you would use with wax or clay.

Another way to do it is to apply paper layer by layer. Glue it to a similar composition, then form it into your desired doll. The good thing about paper is that you can easily use it as an alternative for other Voodoo doll materials, like clay and wax.

Besides the mentioned materials, you can also use modern ones, like foam, polyethylene, and plastic. You can use all the available materials you think you can transform into a doll.

# Steps in Making Voodoo Dolls

Now that you know the materials you can use to create your own voodoo doll, it is time to familiarize yourself with the actual creation process. Here's how you can make one for whatever purpose or intention you have in mind:

### Step 1 – Prepare the Materials

Make an authentic voodoo doll on your own by collecting all the materials you need first. Pick those materials that perfectly suit the purpose or intention you have in mind. You may use any of the materials mentioned earlier.

After that, stuff it with moss. In choosing the material for your doll, go for one to which you are strongly connected. In this case, allow your spirit to serve as your guide. Listen to what your spirit or Lwa is telling you, and you will be able to pick the right materials.

Apart from the materials you have to use for the doll's body, it is also advisable to gather items representing the subject or target of your spell. Remember that Voodoo practitioners strongly believe in sympathetic magic. This means that a human can transfer his energy to any inanimate object he touches or comes in contact with.

So, you can build a link between your target and the doll by collecting any of the target's personal items. These include clothes and hair – both of which are extremely powerful. Any object touched by the person works, too.

### Step 2 – Form the Skeleton

You should then form the doll's skeleton. Note that your goal is to make it feel and look exactly the same as the one you intend to represent, particularly their basic anatomy. In that case, connect a couple of sticks using twine to form the t-shaped skeleton.

If possible, use natural materials for these as this can create an authentic doll. You can use pencils and pick a stick designated for the arms, head, and feet in the absence of branches or wood.

### Step 3 - Stuff the Doll

This is similar to filling a stuffed animal. You have to wrap the formed skeleton using cotton, paper, shredded cloth, or feathers. If you want your Voodoo doll to become even more authentic, then use Spanish moss as stuffing. It is more natural, producing better and more authentic effects.

### Step 4 - Pick the Material for the Skin

Your choice should depend on the actual spell you intend to use. Ensure that the material is large enough as you will be using it to cover the doll entirely. In most cases, this skin is based on fabric. You may also use an organic material or corn husk. Pick the appropriate color, too, as it can greatly influence the spell.

For instance, to cast a spell using the voodoo doll to manifest luck and wealth, choose green. You can also use natural fibers, such as muslin or hemp, to encourage fortune and luck.

### Step 5 - Form the Head, Feet, and Torso

After wrapping your chosen fabric around the skeleton and stuffing, you can start making the head, feet, and torso. You can do so helped by a ribbon or twine. Once done, you can draw the face of the doll.

It should resemble the person who your spell targets, making the doll more effective. For instance, if that person has brown eyes, use brown buttons for the doll's eyes. Use brown yarn for the doll's hair if he has brown hair, too.

### Step 6 - Decorate the Doll

Ensure that the added decorations are based on the specific purpose or intention you have in mind. These added ornaments and decorations can help make your Voodoo doll more powerful. One example would be a dollar bill or coin you should attach to the doll if your purpose is to use it for wealth. To attract love by casting a spell using the Voodoo doll, you can sew on or attach a heart to it.

### Step 7 – Baptize It

The voodoo doll you have made also needs to be baptized. This will let you associate it with that name. It is also the key to turning it into the person you want your spell to target. Baptizing the doll is even more important if your goal is to hex someone. To baptize it, dunk it underwater while stating the verse for baptism.

It is also crucial to purify the doll. Some ways to purify the doll include dissolving sea salt in the water before the baptism, burning incense close to the doll's body so it can absorb it, and burying the doll underground to absorb the natural energy of Mother Nature.

### Step 8 – Visualize

After you have finally created and baptized or purified your doll, you can start the visualization process. Just hold the Voodoo doll you have made, then visualize the end result. To use it to make someone fall for you, then visualize it. If you intend to use it to heal someone, it would be better if the ill person you want to cure is present during the visualization. That way, you can build a stronger connection between him and the doll.

# How to Use the Voodoo Doll

Once you have finally created your Voodoo doll, you can use it for any purpose or intention you wish to come true. It could be love, guidance, empowerment, or healing. You can even use it for cursing, though it is still advisable to remind yourself not to use it to harm anyone. Some of these Voodoo dolls can also be used as talismans and teaching aids.

To be able to use the doll, incorporate the right colors to it. Remember that color has a great influence on the purpose you intend to attain. As a guide, here are the colors and what they can manifest.

- Red – love, power, and attraction
- White – healing, purification, and positivity

- Green – fertility, growth, money, and wealth
- Purple – psychic exploration, spirit realm, and wisdom
- Yellow – confidence and success
- Blue – peace and love
- Black – negativity. This means you can use it to dispel negative energy or for summoning it.

You can also find these colors on needles and pins you can stick into the Voodoo doll so you can make your intention come true. Usually, you can use it to address a specific person's spirit. It summons or calls upon a spirit through a Lwa, making them listen to your plea so you can manifest your wants, desires, and wishes.

To communicate or interact with a person's spirit, pin a personal token or charm to your doll. It could be a piece of clothing, a strand of hair, or a picture. It is possible to talk directly to his spirit through the doll. You may appeal to the spirit, persuade him to do something, or ask questions.

Another practical use of the voodoo doll is to serve as a focus tool designed for meditation, spells, and prayers. To make it work for that specific purpose, put it on your Voodoo altar or shrine so you can easily focus on it whenever you meditate, pray, or cast spells.

Add special items, such as anointing oils, so you can increase its power while also making your message a lot clearer. Another item you can add is candle magic, which works effectively to transmit your message clearly to the spiritual world.

There are several ways for you to use Voodoo dolls. One thing to remember, though, is that they are not completely evil. The majority of the rituals you can do while using the dolls are beneficial to your well-being.

However, several decades back, African slaves used these dolls to defend themselves secretly from their masters. The trauma brought on by that part of the community's history is probably why Voodoo dolls are mistakenly perceived as tools for causing vengeance and harm.

Yes, you can charge it any way you want, but ill-will, harm, and malice should never be part of your intentions. If you use it to cause harm to others, then you will likely gain karmic backlash in the end, like bad luck, conflict, and depression.

Traditionally, a priest or someone in medicine blesses it to carry healing light and positive vibrations and prevent it from being used to cause negativity. Also, try to do the same if you want to make the most out of your Voodoo doll.

# Chapter 8: The Voodoo Way of Life

To be a Voodooist, you should make this religion a part of your life. You have to learn the Voodoo way of life to make it work wonders for you. There are daily routines and practices you have to follow if you want Voodoo to give you the results you want.

Remember that Voodoo requires you to act. You need to act on it as it is the only way to live and breathe the religion. Note that as a Voodoo practitioner, you need to be able to bring its principles to life. You can't just learn it passively. It requires you to participate in its practices actively.

For instance, each ritual and ceremony requires you to take action. You have to act and move. Among the things you have to do are salute, dance, play drums, sing, and draw or trace veves or Voodoo symbols. You will see no member of the community sitting while someone else preaches.

As a member of the Voodoo community, you also have to know that each day of the week will be dedicated to practicing Voodoo. Here's the daily routine that is so typical for most, if not all, Voodoo practitioners:

• **Sunday** – This is considered God's day. However, one thing to note is that Voodoo practitioners differ in terms of what they do on Sundays. Some commit not to perform any form of spiritual work. You will not see them saluting any Lwa and worshipping spirits and other objects.

They focus more on serving just one God as this specific day is so sacred to Him. To do the same, then you can dedicate Sundays as the perfect time to respect, remember, and worship God.

• **Monday** – Many consider this day as the start of the week. Monday is so sacred to the ancestors and Lwas, known as Legba and Gede. Since Monday serves as the week's opening, it is also the best time to take care of the same Lwa you have to care for before moving on to the next.

You can think of it this way. Right after worshipping and focusing on God on Sunday, which is His day, you have to take care of your ancestors. When that happens, you can expect everything to flow more easily, specifically working with the Lwa. It is here where you can expect Gede, along with his ancestors, to come in.

However, before you can call other spirits or Lwa, remember that you have to salute Legba, who serves as the gatekeeper, first. It is in Papa Legba's hands whether he will open up the doors for you or close them.

Once you have the first couple of days set up, you can expect the remaining days of the week to flow naturally. You just have to make sure that your rituals and routines focus on the Lwas or spirits, which are considered the most powerful on those days. Here is a guide:

• **Tuesday** – a sacred day to the spirits who are part of the Petro family. Knowing that, you have to focus your rituals on them, more particularly Ezili Danto.

- **Wednesday** – a sacred day for the Nago nation. Spirits or Lwas in this nation will be more powerful during this day. You can expect supreme power from Ezili Danto, more specifically.

- **Thursday** – This day is meant for the Rada family as the spirits here will likely bring out their superior power.

- **Friday** – This day belongs to Gede, more specifically Brijit and Baron.

- **Saturday** – It is the best day to have a grand ritual or ceremony as it is when all Lwas are powerful.

## Serving the Lwas

One Voodoo routine and ritual you have to follow to ingrain this religion into your life is to serve a Lwa based on his sacred day. There are many ways to achieve such a goal – one of which is to wear the color of a particular Lwa on their day. Another routine you should strictly follow is to observe abstinence on that specific day. Voodoo rituals will also always involve serving them and singing with them throughout the ceremony.

Anyone married to a specific Lwa will have to observe and celebrate that Lwa's sacred day. Here, you can choose to wear specific clothes, prepare your bed in a specific manner, and do things capable of signifying the sacred commitment of the human spouse.

## Worshipping Nature and the Ancestors

For understanding the way of life in the Voodoo community, getting to know more about worshipping nature and the ancestors is a must. Note that the primary belief of most Voodooists is there is only a single Creator, but such a supreme God is distant and can only interact through spirits. Because of that, spirits and spiritual communication are extremely popular in practicing Voodoo.

This belief is one reason why it is extremely important to worship ancestors and nature. As an animist religion, which consecrates a huge community to Lwas or spirits and ancestors, it is truly necessary to learn how to worship them. These ancestors constitute a system composed of religious rites and beliefs mainly used to reinforce the social system and family dependence. It also aims to reinforce voodoo spirits, deities, guardians, and forces of nature.

It is also crucial to worship ancestors as this can also help bring out the power of the spirits. Note that spirits are extremely powerful in the sense they can influence both nature and human existence. Every spirit is responsible for different facets or domains of life. Also, note that some of Voodoo's spirits are believed to be the souls of the departed.

However, it is necessary to worship them. It is a central belief regarding the power of spirits that combine ancestor worship and animism together, allowing the spirits of deceased loved ones, and the spirits of all-natural elements, to become powerful forces for someone to ask for help.

# Daily Devotionals

Voodoo practitioners and devotees are famous for their ability to spend a huge portion of their life worshipping spirits or Lwas. Most offer blood sacrifices, prayers, and thanksgiving to the deities or spirits. They often perform such rituals to find advice, promote good fortune, and build a strong connection with the spiritual realm.

One of the most commonly used routines for Voodooists is to perform daily devotionals. It is a part of the daily life they commit to doing. A lot of Voodooists make it a habit to have a sort of daily devotional. This is especially true for Voodooists who serve the community to obtain their primary source of income. In this daily routine, it is crucial to set the goal of waking up the spirits or Lwas, so they can work with you. Doing daily devotionals the right way is also the key to opening your home and gaining clientele.

It is crucial to create your personal devotion to a specific Lwa every day. You just need to set aside a few minutes, even just five minutes or so, for this daily devotion. Note you may spend even just a short moment praying. You can make it either short or long. It also works well if you intend to get Lwa to work in your everyday life.

Besides the daily devotionals, you can also practice Voodoo through certain routines and rituals, including:

• **Possession, Which is a Sacred Ritual** – This specific ritual requires you to worship the possessed and then listen intently to what they have to say based on the messages of the spirit.

• **Taking Part in Ceremonies** - Ceremonies will always be part of the Voodoo community's routines. We call the Manje Yanm meant to celebrate the yam harvest with the first yam being offered to Lwa Ginen. Note that while this ceremony has no fixed date, you must do it whenever you harvest yam once you become part of the community.

• **Use of Voodoo Dolls** – Discussed in the previous chapter, the voodoo doll is a major part of the community. The goal of this doll is to symbolize or represent people whose energy you intend to influence or affect. As an example, you can create the Voodoo doll to attract someone into your life.

Just put the created doll in your bedroom so you can attract his energy. As a sacred object, you can also use the doll to release positive energy and promote healing and positivity, above many other things.

By practicing Voodoo, you can make positive changes in your life. All it takes is to practice it every day and serve a particular Lwa. As a way of life, this religion helps remove obstacles that may block your path toward success and happiness. Avoid using the Voodoo practice to hurt others, though.

To make it a part of your life, reflect on how exactly you can use it. You have to know how you can get the support and guidance of Lwas and deities. That way, you can also gain access to positive energy, making it possible for you to manifest only the good things in your life. Avoid being negative when casting your spells, for instance, as it may only cause you to encourage negativity instead of positive things.

## Voodoo vs. Christian Traditions

As mentioned in previous chapters, Voodoo is a syncretized religion as it also has a link to Christian traditions. However, some things make the two distinctive, particularly in their traditions and rituals.

For instance, most Christians and Roman Catholics worship their God and saints in the church, cathedrals, chapels, basilicas, and personal dwellings. Voodoo devotees, on the other hand, worship their God and Lwas in temples and use altars. The two are the same, though, in the sense they need to worship higher beings and deities (the Lwas for Voodoo and saints for Christians, usually).

Voodoo and Christian practices also have similarities and differences. Christians, for instance, believe in praying and worshipping in church. They also practice reading the Bible and following the sacraments, communion, and acts of charity. Meanwhile, you can see Voodoo traditions focusing not only on prayer, daily devotion, and healing but also on witchcraft. Their traditions also include blessings, and they have clear distinctions between good and evil.

The main purpose of Christianity is to love God while obeying his commandments. The religion also puts more emphasis on spreading the Gospel to save others. In the Voodoo community, you can see their traditions and practices focusing more on honoring God and the Lwas. They also emphasize more on celebrating and honoring life. With that in mind, your daily life should focus more on healing and initiation if you intend to practice Voodoo.

# Chapter 9: Invocation and Summoning Ritual

Among the most vital aspects of the Voodoo religion are invocation and summoning rituals. These rituals aim to call upon a specific Lwa based on the occasion being celebrated or the specific intention of the Voodoo practitioner doing the ritual. One of the most interesting things about Voodoo is the strong relationship between the dead and the living. It is life itself that also gives birth to Lwas and spirits that the followers have to summon, depending on their intentions.

Contrary to what other people believe, though, invoking or summoning spirits does not necessarily mean you must call upon the evil ones. It is even possible for you to invoke peaceful spirits, including deities, ancestors, and gods and goddesses. You can do that by chanting sincere prayers and peaceful responses.

Note that to invoke and summon a specific spirit or Lwa, music and chanting should always be present. The reason is that the spirits respond a lot better to dance rhythms, music, and chanting, is that doing this shows how the devotees worship, honor, and respect them.

Music and chants are necessary to address the spirit with respect, together with sincere prayers. With this included, there is a higher chance for you to succeed in bringing the spirit to life and allowing them to guide you throughout your everyday life and actions.

The act of summoning and invoking spirits can be considered as a highly advanced type of spell. The reason is that it requires you to call upon a higher being in the form of the spirit or Lwa and the deity. With that in mind, you should never take this entire process lightly. Avoid invoking an entity or spirit who does not want to be summoned lightly.

If you intend to summon a high-frequency spirit or entity, conduct all the necessary research about it first. Frequency, in this case, refers to the specific vibrational level through which an entity or spirit operates.

## Importance of Purpose and Intention

Aside from music and chanting that serve as avenues to show respect to the Lwas, it is also necessary for you to have a distinct intention or purpose for summoning and invoking a Lwa. As a beginner, you have to know exactly your purpose or intention for summoning a spirit. There should be a distinct goal or purpose in mind. Knowing your exact purpose will be easier for you to strengthen your skills and focus on your attempt or the entire ritual.

Also, remember that the Lwa you are trying to summon will most likely listen if you can draw their attention to your presence. The invocation's actual purpose will also clearly show you the exact Lwa you should call upon. You can summon a specific spirit or Lwa for purposes like wealth, relationships, health, and social status. You can also invoke one to help you handle a certain problem.

Ensure that you have a good and valuable reason for summoning the spirit. Imagine them as grumpy people who do not want to be disturbed when asleep. With that said, your reason should be really good for calling upon them. You need not be in a life-or-death situation when doing so, but your purpose should be a good excuse to bother and wake them up. Only summon them when you require their help and assistance for a problem you can't solve independently.

# How to Invoke or Summon the Right Lwa

To invoke the correct spirit or Lwa, you have to look for a summoning ritual specifically intended for them. You can learn some rituals and magic spells from books and other sources. You can also design and make your own. When choosing or creating rituals, remember that it often consists of three basics steps – building the most suitable atmosphere for the ritual, getting into the trance state, and summoning/invoking and interacting with the spirit.

### Create the Perfect Atmosphere

Building the perfect atmosphere for your rituals should be one thing you have to do when invoking Lwas. If you are still new to this realm, you may wonder why rituals often look kind of sinister and scary. The reason behind this is that it builds up the right atmosphere that encourages the spirits to come out.

This first step aims to create a specific atmosphere in the area designated for the ritual. It is also crucial for the participants of the ritual to have the right mindset. You have to create a mindset of uniformity, self-sacrifice, and discipline and show it in the way you dress for the ritual and set up the designated place for it.

Now, the question is, what kind of atmosphere should you aim for when performing invocation and summoning rituals? The answer is an atmosphere capable of separating you from your mundane daily reality. You have to be in a different atmosphere – one that can convert your mind into a more spiritual state.

### Getting Into the Trance State

The atmosphere you have created for the ritual should be the one that will bring you to the right trance state. Here, you will need to use the right sounds, objects, colors, and patterns to connect with your spiritual nature. Reaching the trance state, in this case, does not mean you must get rid of your sense of reality completely.

What you should be after is a theta brainwave state – one like you usually enter as you are falling asleep. It refers to the quiet area between being awake and experiencing your dreams. You have to penetrate this state as this is the most appropriate mental state for spell casting and conjuration.

For you to reach this state of mind, you can use one or a combination of these tools:

- **Veves/Sigils** – The veves or the Voodoo symbols we have discussed in one chapter of this book should be used to get into the trance state. Veves refer to the symbols of various spirits as previously discussed. Used for centuries, you can use them for your summoning rituals by looking directly at them.

   You can draw the veve yourself while the ritual is ongoing. Drawing it on your own is beneficial as it can give you a more trance-inducing experience, increasing your chances of getting into the desired trance state fast.

- **Enns** – These refer to sound frequencies that one can use when connecting with spirits and deities. You can chant these *enns* or use them as silent mantras. You may use them based on your discretion, provided the end result is the trance state.

- **Candles** – You also need to have candles around. This is crucial as you need to gaze at the flames of the candles to build a theta state. The reason is that it will let you focus your attention on the flame while also feeling relaxed. Another way to use the candles is to visualize the specific spirit you intend to invoke or summon. Just imagine this spirit manifesting in the flame, and you will have an easier time entering the trance state.

• **Some Pointy Objects** – Some examples are sword, dagger, and wand. They often serve as extensions of your hand. This is necessary as extending your hand will let you channel energy more effectively. It is like that scenario of you hitting someone using any of the mentioned objects.

However, the major difference is you do not use the objects for fighting or combat. What you do, instead, is charge a specific space or object by sending magical energy to it. You can charge a veve or sigil, magical circle, mirror, or anything that symbolizes the spirit you are summoning or invoking.

• **Magic Circle** – Sometimes, you may need to create a magic circle on the floor. You can mark a circle on the floor, which serves as the exact spot where you can trap the spirit you summon. You may also use this magical circle to protect where you stand or sit while you let the spirit linger or stay outside.

If you plan to use this element for your summoning rituals, remember that it usually requires you to make two circles. One should be for you, while the other should be for the spirit. The good thing about the circle is that it can create a form of separation.

It is great as the spirits may interfere with all the present energies in the area and people. Note, however, that using a magic circle is optional. A lot of those who regularly summon Lwas do not even use this element in their rituals.

• **Meditation** – You can also meditate to reach the trance state. One advantage of this technique is that you do not have to prepare ritual objects for it. The only things you need to reach the trance state through meditation are concentration and a clear mind. Meditate for around thirty minutes to cleanse your mind and get rid of all unnecessary thoughts, making it possible for you to reach the trance state quickly.

Using any or a combination of these tools and techniques, you can bring your mind into a trance-like state, making it possible for you to gain better results from the ritual. You may also use other items, like magic robes, gemstones, and crystal balls. The color of the items also matters a lot. For instance, you can use the color red to invoke warlike spirits. The goal is to use the elements with their corresponding elements and colors to create a trance-inducing state and an appropriate ritualistic atmosphere.

### Invoking the Spirit

Now that you have prepared the perfect atmosphere for the ritual and reached the trance state, you can invoke the spirit or Lwa. The state you are in will make it easier for you to interact with spirits. This is mainly because your consciousness is already at that point where you can respond more effectively to such influences. Your goal is to invoke or summon the spirit in such a way it enters your body, allowing you to have its traits.

Avoid mistaking invocation for possession, though, as the two are different. If you are possessed, then it means that the spirit controls you. Invocation, on the other hand, leaves you in control. However, you will have many personality changes since you are already receiving the traits of your summoned spirit.

There, you should start calling for your chosen spirit. You can do it by saying formal incantations from various sources or writing your own rituals and using them. If you are gifted, then you can also rely on any form of inspiration that comes to you during the entire procedure.

It would be best for you to be more creative in your rituals as spirits prefer them. Ensure that you also make the entire ritual a unique and personal experience for you. Once you have successfully summoned the spirit, remember that you can command it. Avoid the mistake of humbling yourself too much. It would not be a great idea to act like a servant or slave when trying to communicate what you want.

Command the spirit as you are a conjurer. You are the creator or god of the entity you have summoned to this plane of reality. Avoid disrespecting the spirit, though. You can command it while still acting with respect, not only to the spirit but also to yourself.

Once you have successfully communicated your desire and got what you want, feel free to end the ritual. What you should do is to thank the spirit. Express how thankful you are for their presence, giving you answers to your questions, and providing guidance. Ensure that the candles you light up during the ritual continue burning until they go out on their own. After that, you can dispose of them. Avoid reusing the candles or any other items you have used for this ritual for another.

# Basic Invocation Ritual

Now that you are aware of the usual steps for invoking spirits, here is a basic ritual you can follow.

### Things You Need:

- Silver or white candle

- Gift for the spirit – You can offer anything as a gift, but you have to make sure that it fits and represents the spirit you wish to summon. Some great examples are drink, food, and tobacco.

- 1 cup of salt

- Sage smudge stick

### Spirit Invocation Instructions:

1.      Get rid of all the negative energies surrounding you. A wise tip is to prepare a cleansing bath. Just run lukewarm water in a tub, then add the salt to it. Soak your body in it for 20 minutes or so. After that, dry off, then wear something comfortable.

2.      Cast a circle and ask for blessings.

3. Light the sage. Then smudge yourself as well as the area inside the circle. It is helpful to remove the negative energies still there. Allow the sage to continue burning after that.

4. Put the silver or white candle in a holder. After that, put your offerings or gifts around it.

5. Close your eyes, then breathe deeply. Your goal should be to focus more on being welcoming and open with your eyes closed and while taking deep breaths. Light the candle, then recite your prepared incantation or ritual.

6. Wait for the spirit to come to you. If you have successfully summoned the spirit, then ask your questions or request guidance or any other form of help you are seeking.

# Invoking Papa Legba

Here is also an example of summoning a specific Lwa in the Voodoo community. In this case, it would be Papa Legba who you should invoke first as he is the gatekeeper of the spiritual world. It would be best if you knew exactly how you could summon Papa Legba, as he will be the one to open the gates for the spirits to come to you.

Here's what you will need for this invocation ritual:

- Red and black candle
- Rum
- Three coins
- Cigar
- Sugarcane juice
- Cookies and other sweets
- Groundnuts
- Veve of Papa Legba

**Procedure:**

1.      Put everything on the altar, then light all the things that have to be lit, like the red and black candle and the cigar. Begin meditating.

2.      If you feel ready, summon or call Papa Legba. One great thing about summoning Papa Legba is that language will never be an issue. Do not worry about whether Papa Legba understands you. Summon him by reciting or singing his prayer.

"Papa Legba, open the gate for me.

Antibon Legba, please open the gate.

Legba open the gate for me, and I will thank

the Lwa when I return."

3.      Observe his response. If you feel like he is already around, you can ask for his help and guidance. Communicate with him, just like when talking to a friend. He will listen to whatever you want to say. Allow yourself to open up to him. After that, ask him respectfully to open up the gates so the other Lwas or spirits will come out. Be specific when mentioning the Lwa you intend to talk to.

4.      After you send your request, offer him the items you have prepared on the altar. This should also be the perfect time to begin invoking the specific Lwa you wish to interact with. Remember, though, that each Lwa requires a different ritual. The reason is these spirits have different preferences.

5.      Once you have successfully completed your invocation rituals to your desired Lwa, express your gratitude to Papa Legba. Thank him for listening to you and allowing you to speak to a specific spirit. Then ask Papa Legba to close the gate as he returns to his world.

After completing the ritual, it would be best to gather all the offerings you have prepared. Bring them to a crossroad so you can drop off Papa Legba together with the gifts you offer him. Leave the offerings beneath a tree close to the crossroad or at the side.

## Some Warnings to Keep in Mind

Regardless of what you are looking for, whether it's answers to questions, guidance, or help with any aspect of your life, you have to use the invocation ritual with caution. Do extensive research before you even start. Avoid rushing the process so you prevent mistakes that will lead to irreparable harm to you or anyone. Remember that while this activity is rewarding, it also has consequences if you do not do it correctly.

# Chapter 10: Voodoo Cleansing and Protection Spells

The Voodoo spells you can cast may also promote cleansing. Remember that several waves and energies are surrounding you. Some of these energies are positive, while the others are negative. It is the reason you have to learn a few cleansing spells. You can cast them to bring more positive energies into your life and your household while getting rid of the negative.

## Voodoo Cleansing Spells for Your Home

You may want to cast Voodoo cleansing spells if you feel like your home is already becoming full of negativity. Cleansing, in this case, refers to rituals you can perform to purify your space. It aims to eliminate stagnant, malicious, and negative energies and entities.

Several Voodoo practitioners perform cleansing rituals before casting spells because they fear any negative presence. They also do it solely for their home's general upkeep. You can cleanse all spaces and objects in your home. The people inside your home can even be cleansed. Usually, you will need to use cleansing tools that are personal for you for the spells and rituals to become even more effective.

There could be various reasons for you to cleanse your home. It could be either positive or negative. One reason is that you may just have moved to your home and wish to celebrate your new space by anointing, blessing, and purifying it.

Another potential reason is the presence of negative energy in your house which you want to eliminate or clear. Negative energy can be linked to spirits. It could be that someone died in the house naturally, by choice (suicide), or through a murder. Note, however, those are not the only reasons for negative energy to come out. Human behaviors may also trigger it.

For instance, if something negative happens inside the home due to the behavior of someone living there, you can't clean this negative energy unless he completely stops the negative behavior. With that said, you have to discover first if anyone in your household contributes to the piling up of negative energy before casting Voodoo home cleansing spells.

Among the scenarios that may require you to do the Voodoo cleansing for your home would be:

- Living in a house that has a violent and disturbing history
- Traumatic events that happened inside the household
- Recent burglary
- Spooky feelings and vibes inside the house
- Constant arguments with partner or family members with no viable reason
- Restless sleep
- Crying with no reason
- Sudden illnesses

• Desire to manifest luck, love life, good relationships, and a new job or house

• Desire to improve an area or aspect of your life

If you have experienced any of the mentioned scenarios, you may want to consider casting Voodoo cleansing spells and rituals. Before that, though, remember these tips:

• **Clean Your House Thoroughly** - Remove all junk from your homes as well as anything inside it that is depressing. Clean all parts of your home, including the garage, attic, and basement. After that, gather a lot of things you find pleasing and let them surround you. It could be pictures of your loved ones, attractive flowers, and your favorite ornaments. Surround yourself with uplifting and pleasing things so you can begin inviting positive energy.

• **Allow Sunlight, Fresh Air, and Other Forms of Nature to Penetrate** - Allow your home to receive natural light or sunlight for a few days before the ritual or spell. This is necessary to let fresh air get in, too, which is a huge help when moving energy. The sunlight will always have a cleansing and revitalizing effect. If possible, put some living plants around your home. Their nature is known for emitting energy healing traits.

• **Open All Doors** - Ensure you also open every door in your home. It could be your house's main door or your French windows, closet, drawer, cabinet, oven, and microwave, among many others. It is the key to removing negative and dark energy and taking them out from hiding.

• **Walk Counterclockwise** - Before doing your house cleansing rituals and spells, make sure that you are walking counterclockwise - walking to the right while being close to the walls all the time. It is necessary as this direction can help to banish and drive out all negative energies. After clearing a specific room, ensure that you use the same door you used to enter to exit if that space has at least two doors.

## Using Candles for Cleansing

To get rid of negative energy from your home and any earth-bound souls staying there, white candles combined with house cleansing prayers can help. White symbolizes enlightenment, and the candles in this color can draw such a form of enlightenment from the light. A blessed herbal candle containing sage, cypress, and lemongrass blend may also be used as an alternative.

To use the candle, set your intention of removing negative energy and dark entities from your home. Light the candle, then say your chosen house cleansing prayer. This prayer could be something like, "Dear Supreme God, remove all negative energies from this home. Bless and cover it with your pure and genuine white light of protection and love."

Repeat this prayer several times to affirm your desire and intention. You can expect the light from the candle to respond to you and guide you.

## Using Sea Salt for Cleansing

Sea salt is also another effective tool for cleansing your home. It allows you to remove all forms of disturbance and dark energy from your home safely and effectively. The good thing about sea salt is that it has a strong cleaning power, which significantly improves its cleansing ability. You can use it for your home and office cleansing rituals. Here's how.

1. Clear your mind from all thoughts. Set an intention to remove negative energy from your home.

2. Spread the sea salt on your home's exteriors. Spread it on every window, step, and doorway. When doing this, say this spell loudly:

106

"Remove all negative energies and entities from this place.

Only those who love purely may enter this home".

3. Repeat it until you have spread the salt completely around your house.

4. Put some sea salt into small bowls. If possible, fill each bowl, then put one in every room in your house. Let it stay there for at least 24 hours so it can absorb all dark and negative entities.

5. Once the 24-hour period is up, throw the sea salt away. Make sure that the used salt is no longer part of your house.

# Using Incense for Cleansing

It is also possible for you to take advantage of incense's vibrational frequency to help remove house-bound spirits and dark entities. Using incense in cleansing and clearing your home will allow you to deal with a certain vibration and universal force, which can naturally enhance the vibes within your home.

Sandalwood is an example of incense you can use for house cleaning. It works to awaken your chi or life force. Other great choices are sage and lavender. To cleanse using your choice of incense, do the following:

1.	Open all windows, doors, drawers, closets, and any other item in your home with doors like the oven and microwave.

2.	Build your strong intention of clearing your place before the actual home cleansing.

3.	Once you already have your intention, you can burn a stick of incense. Put it in the specific room in your house you think requires thorough cleansing.

4.	Walk counterclockwise. You can do that by keeping close to the walls and the right side when walking.

5.    Wave the lighted incense beneath your furniture, bedding, and around the walls of your closets. Say the prayer or mantra to remove all negative energies and unwanted vibrations from your home.

# How to Cleanse Your Body

Note that your body may also be filled with many negative energies, spirits, and vibrations, just like your home. Fortunately, you can also cleanse it helped by Voodoo spells. Here are a couple of ways to do so:

### Cleansing Bath Spell

For this spell to work, you need a white candle and seven dried dandelion flowers. You can cast this spell through these steps:

1. Prepare yourself to take a warm bath.

2. Get the dried dandelion flowers, then crumble them in the water. Recite this spell seven times as you drop each flower:

"Bare vindeca bare!"

3. Get the candle and light it up. Allow yourself to get completely immersed in the water. Then say the following spell seven times:

"By virtue of the Supreme God and the Lwas. Bare and Vindeca.

Purify my body. Bare and Vindeca.

Purge my soul. Set it free from evil. Protect it from evil spirits. So be it."

4. Use the water to snuff the candle.

5. Spend a few minutes meditating. Visualize your body. Imagine it glowing with light. After that, you can complete the ritual by getting yourself out of the water.

# Cleansing Water Spell

One advantage of this spell is that it is something that you can do quickly. It works for beginners, too. Among the things you need for this spell are one glass of water, coarse salt, and three white candles. To do it, here are the steps:

1.   Form a triangle from coarse salt. Put the glass with water inside the triangle.

2.   Place each candle in the triangle's vertices. Light them all.

3.   Recite the following ritual afterward:

"Supreme God, Father of the Universe, purifies this water.

May it be purified in your name

Purify this liquid, make it blood, make it holy.

How sacred is the blood of your Divine Son, as your word is sacrosanct.

Word of love and justice. Forever and ever. So be it!"

4.   Drink the water and allow all the candles to burn out.

# Voodoo Spell of Protection

Besides being useful for the body and home cleansing, you can also cast Voodoo spells for protection. It is great, especially if you know exactly how you can protect yourself if another practitioner hexes you. A hex refers to a curse or magical attack, which may be intended to cause you harm. Note that despite the constant reminder that Voodoo should not be used to harm someone, there are still a few practitioners who do it.

There are two forms of curse or magical attack that may be used against you. It could be a direct curse or hex, operated against you helped by the suitable cursed material. This can be of a distinct nature, like herbs, menstrual blood, or powdered bones of anyone who has died. It can represent a sensitive instrument that allows evil to exercise power.

The cursed material is then sent to you in a few ways – adding it to your drinks or foods or being in contact with an object close to it. One example is your braided hair combined with blood and other kinds of materials placed within a mattress or cushion.

There is also what we call an indirect curse, which occurs via transference. This means resorting to certain things and objects representing you. It could be your clothes, puppets, or pictures.

## How to Break a Curse or Hex

You can also break or purge a curse or hex and cleanse yourself, which is a good thing, especially if you never want to harm yourself. One way to do so is to use an amulet. Usually, this involves taking objects properly spellbound, personalized, and prepared with you all the time. It helps to ward off evil desires and vibrations. You can expect such elements to weaken the spell's effects, preventing it from hurting you.

Some of the amulets you can use for protection are crystals, a cross, or a pentagram. You can put an amulet or two inside your pocket or wear one around your neck. Other ways to break a curse or hex are:

• **Use Magic Herbs and Salt Baths** – You can use these items to cleanse and ward off the intentions of evil, particularly from those that intend to destroy you. Perform this ritual by preparing the appropriate atmosphere. You can do so by lighting a few candles then letting your bathtub filled with warm water.

Attract good fortune by thinking of pleasant and positive thoughts when doing this routine. You can make its healing power even stronger by adding or spraying it with salt, basil, absinthe, patchouli, and hyssop.

• **Burn Salt** – You can also remove a curse by burning salt. It cleanses and purifies, allowing another cycle of life to start. It also helps maintain the beauty of life. Spiritually, this technique can purify and neutralize psychic and negative energies in different cultures.

To protect yourself from curses and hex, or avoid them as much as possible, know how to burn salt correctly. The first thing to do is light up a fire-based wherever spot is convenient for you. It could be in your fireplace or burning charcoals spread on the ground.

Get some coarse salt, around a handful of it. Think of each negativity you wish to remove. After that, rub the salt on your skin for purification. After that, throw the rubbed salt into the embers or fire. To be honest, this technique can either produce fast and dry results or progressive and slow ones. Do which one you feel is ideal for you.

The fire from the candle works to burn the salt. It causes the salt to burst then raises the flame. By completing this ritual, you can finally set yourself free from all negative energies and the hex or curse being cast on you.

• **Burn Incense** – You may also want to burn incense to break a hex or curse. The good thing about incense is that it has a genuine cleansing effect. It breaks the spell or curse then throws out bad energy. It would be much better for you to use the incense and other herbs to significantly enhance its power.

To take advantage of it, but the incense together with the herbs you intend to use. Use a thread to tie them together. With that, you can expect them to be burned thoroughly and much faster. After consuming everything through the fire, you will notice its positive effects. Also, it helps to get a few branches of plants like sage and put them between the layers of your clothes. Doing so can help to ward off evil spirits.

Before taking advantage of any of the techniques mentioned for your next ritual, it also helps to remind yourself of:

- Avoid eating red meat.

- Avoid drinking coffee for a couple of weeks before the ritual and two more weeks after that.

- Smoking and alcohol are not allowed.

- Attend rituals and ceremonies in temples.

You can do several things to protect yourself from danger, especially from those who intend to harm you through magical attack, curse, or hex.

# Chapter 11: Voodoo Love Spells

Voodoo magic is also so impressive that it can help you attain happiness regardless of where you are. There are Voodoo love spells that you can use to find love. One great thing about these Voodoo spells is that they are effective, plus they work fast. These spells are so swift that right after you cast them on your desired target, you can expect your intention to travel directly to their conscience.

With that, your target will surely develop a different idea, perception, and thought about you right away. Also, Voodoo's love spells can be used for a wide range of love-related motives we will discuss in this chapter.

## Voodoo Spell to Make Someone Fall in Love

You will be using a Voodoo doll for this spell. This doll will represent the specific person you are targeting. By casting the spell, you can change how your target looks at you. The spell even aims to make your target fall in love with you. Here are the things you need for this spell:

- Voodoo doll representing your desired partner
- A personal item from your desired partner

- Something personal that you own
- White paper
- 3 ribbons – 1 each in the colors black, white, and red
- White candle
- Red ink with a feather serving as a pen

Create the Voodoo doll on your own using materials like clay, wax, or a piece of fabric you sew by hand. Put something used by your intended partner into the doll. It could be their hair or nail clipping. You also have to integrate something from you into the doll. Carve the name of your subject into the doll. Once you have prepared the Voodoo doll, you can start casting this spell.

**Instructions:**

1.     Do this love spell on the day after the New Moon. This often happens on a Friday.

2.     Prepare your Voodoo altar. You can do so by using a wooden match to light up the candle.

3.     Get the three ribbons, then use them to wrap or cover the Voodoo doll. Ensure that you knot the ribbons together. While wrapping and knotting the doll with the ribbons, make sure to say the following aloud:

"These tapes tie you up

and weave your heart to mine."

4.     Get the red ink and paper. Use it to write your target's name. Place the paper with the written name on your altar.

5.     Put the Voodoo doll on a sheet, then blow out the candle.

6.     Light the candle again the following night.

7.     Take the Voodoo doll, then put it closer to the flame. You should then say,

"For you, I crave

for me, you burn."

8.      Let the Voodoo doll rest on the prepared sheet. Do not blow out the candle. Let it continue burning for one hour or so.

9.      Wrap your Voodoo doll using an object in red, then store it in a place that makes it safe.

# Voodoo Spell to Bring Back Your Ex

If you still love your ex and you truly want to get back together with them, then know there is also a Voodoo spell you can use for that. For this specific love spell, you will need:

• Two voodoo dolls made by you – one is representing you while the other representing your ex.

• White candle

• Red candle

• Some offerings, like fruit and chocolates

• Red string

**Instructions:**

1.      Light the white candle before doing the love spell.

2.      Let your mind relax, then do not let your eyes look directly at the flame.

3.      Think about your happy moments together and reminisce. Doing this is important as it helps build a positive vibe capable of getting rid of bad energy that can positively influence your love life.

4.      Light the red candle, then put it beside the white candle.

5.      Prepare the necessary offerings. They could be chocolates, fruit, or perfume. Put these offerings on a plate.

6.      Create a couple of dolls, too. They should symbolize you and your ex. Then allow the two dolls to sit at the table. Ensure that they are facing each other.

7.      Say your prayer or cast your spell, just like the one in the previous chapter. The spell or prayer's intent should be to bring your ex back to you and make your relationship and connection stronger this time.

8.      Tie the dolls together using a red string. Make sure that the faces of the dolls touch each other. After that, hide the dolls in a secure place. Blow out the candles once done.

# Voodoo Break-Up Spell

If you are no longer happy with your romantic partner, but you have a hard time breaking up with them, then there is a voodoo spell that can help you. You can also use this spell to make a couple of break up. Some things you need for this purpose are:

- Black candle

- 7 nails

- Recent pictures of the couple you wish to break up – If it is your romance you want to break, then prepare your own picture and that of your partner.

  - 2 tbsps. cayenne powder

  - 1 tbsp. garlic powder

  - 2 tbsps. mustard seeds

  - 1 cup

  - Vinegar

  - Salt

  - A small bowl

  - A string

• A sheet of paper

**Instructions:**

1.      Use vinegar to anoint the black candle.

2.      Get the nails and use them to poke the black candle. This can divide the candle into seven even or equal parts. The seventh pin or nail should be down at the bottom.

3.      Mix the salt, mustard seeds, cayenne pepper, and garlic powder in a small bowl.

4.      Place the paper in front of the black candle you prepared. Light it up.

5.      Put the pictures over the sheet of paper.

6.      Call upon a spirit and ask for help. Be forthright and honest when petitioning a spirit and seeking his help.

7.      Get the lighted candle, then let the candle drip up to 9 drops of wax onto each picture. Sprinkle the mixture on top. Allow the candle to burn until it gets to the first nail. Snuff it out.

8.      Take the first pin out of the candle the following day. Place this pin over the pictures. After that, light the black candle again. Do the same steps when it is time to take the candle, then drip the same number of wax drops onto the pictures. However, remember this time, let the candle burn to the next nail - after which, you have to snuff it out again.

9.      Do the same on the remaining pins or nails. Repeat the steps for seven days. The 7th day should serve as the final ritual. Here, you will have to wrap the contents together with the pictures by tying them securely with paper.

10.     Once done, you can also burn the doll and its contents while the ritual is still ongoing. You can then bury the ashes next to a tree or burn the doll in a cauldron. In this case, you must throw the ashes into the wind.

# Attract Love With a Gris-Gris Bag

You can also attract new love through a Voodoo spell that involves the use of a gris-gris bag. Know this bag is extremely powerful for drawing out a new love. It would be best for this gris-gris bag to be constructed out of red fabric because aside from being powerful, it also works effectively for casting spells designed to attract love.

For this purpose, you need to gather all the items you have to put inside the bag to make the love spell work. These include:

• Something designed to help the energy connect to you – This could be a nail, body fluid, or hair.

• Herbs linked to attracting new love - Among the herbs you can use for this purpose are lavender, cinnamon, patchouli, catnip, basil, vanilla beans, daisy, valerian, and chili pepper.

• Stones capable of drawing love, like ruby, pearl, emerald, rose quartz, and rough diamonds.

**Instructions:**

1.	Set the casting of the love spell at the appropriate time and day. The best time to do it is usually on a Friday night. It should be on the moon's waxing phase, preferably Venus' planetary hour.

2.	Put everything you wish to use in the bag inside a bowl. Ensure that you choose those that are truly powerful in attracting love.

3.	Place your right hand on top of the bowl. Your goal is to let the energy flow into the items inside.

4.	Picture vividly the kind of love you wish to attract and accomplish using the gris-gris bag. This should take around 20 minutes. Your goal is to let your mind clearly see the end result as it can motivate you.

5.     Put several drops of magnet oil into the bag every Friday. Once you feel comfortable with how it manifests your desire, you can bury it in the earth.

# A Warning When Casting Voodoo Love Spells

One thing to remember for casting love spells is that you should avoid using them to harm someone. Note that voodoo attraction love spells require physical transmission by using items and objects that belong to the person subjected to the spell.

Despite being unique, the spell's final results should adhere to all the love spell principles. Some rules and principles you have to follow include:

- Not harming anyone
- Not causing negative side effects for the long term
- Not deceiving the subject

Also, it is necessary to make sure that the strongest spirit present when casting the love spell is that of the ancestors. Their power should be enough to remove all obstacles associated with love. Remember that while Voodoo spells are mainly designed to attract love, others also aim to rekindle the flame.

Another thing to remember is that casting Voodoo spells will always have risks. For instance, if you cast a love spell on someone, remember that it will cause your soul to become bound to them forever. With that said, avoid using a love spell on someone who you just lust after without the intention of being with them forever.

Most of these love spells will bind you. It would be like making an oath to the spirits or ethereal energy patterns you are serious about producing powerful love energy – one that the entire universe can take advantage of only if the spirits you summon change the material plane's energy in your favor. Your goal, therefore, is to make the results lasting, especially if you are after attracting the love of your life.

Overall, your goal should be to produce effects that will harm no one. Remember that if you use spells that harbor bad intentions, then it will likely turn into a self-curse, *so be extra careful.*

# Chapter 12: Ceremonies and Festivals

As a form of belief system and religion, Voodoo also has its own ceremonies and festivals. They have their own holidays and religious celebrations. Some of these events are their unique spin on the holidays and events honored by other religions, especially Christianity and Roman Catholicism. The fact that Voodoo has already become an official religion since 2003 gives the priests in this community the right and authority to hold baptismal and wedding ceremonies, too.

When trying to learn about the popular ceremonies and festivals, note that it encompasses various aspects derived from Haiti's original inhabitants and the African freed slaves, Voodoo folklore, and Roman Catholicism. The following are just a few of the many ceremonies, festivals, and celebrations enjoyed by the Voodoo community.

# Mange Loa

Mango Loa refers to a Voodoo ceremony, which involves a huge feast of all Lwas. This means it involves feeding the Lwas or deities and spirits. Any Voodoo ceremony that requires animal sacrifices and offerings is considered as a Mange Loa. During this ceremony, a lot of offerings will be served to the Lwas.

Aside from animal offerings, like chickens, bulls, and birds, the community will also offer cakes, syrups, and drinks to the Lwa. This celebration often takes place during the 2nd to 3rd week of January every year. Devotees and followers of the Voodoo religion strongly believe that the powers of Lwas increase significantly when celebrating this event.

# Ouidah Voodoo Festival

Happening every 10th of January, the annual Ouidah Voodoo festival is a national celebration in Benin, honoring the traditional religion and its cults. It is even considered the largest gathering of all Voodoo devotees and practitioners in the world. It has the same level of importance as the celebration of Christmas to Christians.

Fortunately, you can attend this event even if you are not a full-blown Voodoo practitioner. You can just enjoy and observe how they celebrate this event. Certain aspects of this festival are not suitable for those with a faint heart, but it is a great way for you to become more enlightened about this misunderstood religion.

During this celebration, expect to see the ritualistic animal sacrifices made by practitioners. Another unique and controversial act during this event that may not be for the weak and squeamish is a sacrifice involving a priest ripping the chicken's neck using his teeth.

This event will also open up some markets full of wood carvings, masks, and fetishes. You will also notice women dressing themselves up with vivid rainbow colors. You may want to participate in this celebration, especially to grab the chance to witness the region's traditional and unique yet controversial culture.

# Fat Gede

Also called the Day of the Dead, the Fat Gede is an annual national holiday in Haiti, the counterpart of All Saints' and All Souls' Day in the Roman Catholic religion. This event is celebrated on November 1 and 2, similar to the dates used in the Catholic religion. This is the time when Voodoo followers honor their dead ancestors.

Just like Catholics, Voodoo practitioners also tend to visit cemeteries to pray. They also light candles and offer flowers, drinks, and food to their departed loved ones. One thing that makes it distinctive from the celebration of Catholics is that Voodooists tend to continue the event in their Voodoo temples called peristyles. They celebrate this day with dancing and rituals for the whole night.

# Bath of Christmas

Another great example of syncretizing Catholic celebrations with Voodoo is the Bath of Christmas, also celebrated by Voodoo devotees and practitioners every December 25. Some Voodoo houses celebrate Christmas Eve (Dec. 24), while other places do it for three days – from December 24 to 26.

This celebration involves Voodoo practitioners rubbing themselves using medical creams. They also rub talismans on their body to attain fortune, luck, and protection. The entire celebration also involves sacrificing animals, like pigs, turkeys, and goats, to honor a Lwa.

One great thing about Christmas Baths for Voodoo is that they are naturally cleansing. They also recognize how powerful these baths are as they can remove all negativity, restraints, curses, and evil spirits lurking around you.

During this event, you must summon and call upon the spirits to integrate their energy into the bath. Aside from sacrifices and offerings, it also involves singing and dancing to heat up the Christmas bath. This makes it more effective in washing out all the things that bind and restrict you, including doubts, aggression, anger, and limitations. This results in you becoming a more renewed person with a lot of potential.

# Voodoo Fest

Another famous celebration that is part of the Voodoo tradition is the Voodoo Fest, which happens every October 31. In most cases, the celebration is a multi-day art and music festival that everyone can participate in for free. This annual festival celebrates Voodoo's several significant contributions to the culture and traditions in New Orleans.

It primarily aims to honor the ancestors and Lwas. It also intends to educate everyone regarding this religion while preserving and celebrating the distinctive cultural and spiritual New Orleans heritage. The Voodoo Fest is a fun and exciting celebration with plenty of interesting activities, including music and arts.

This event also exhibits several educational and cultural presentations, doll making and drumming workshops, and consultations with the leading practitioners of Voodoo in the city. You can expect this to be a fun and exciting day with rituals for ancestral healing.

# Gran Bois

Another Voodoo holiday with a mark in the community is the Gran Bois. This holiday pays tribute to Grand Bois, its namesake that means great wood. It is nature's elemental power with a strong relationship to herbs, medicinal plants, and trees. Grand Bois is also considered the counterpart of St. Sebastian in the Catholic religion, who was venerated as the protector of illnesses. The holiday dedicated to Grand Bois will involve many offerings, including herbs, spiced rum, and honey.

# A Voodoo Calendar

Besides the famous festivals, holidays, and events that honor the Voodoo religion mentioned in this chapter, here are other activities and events that all Voodoo practitioners and devotees observe every year:

| | |
|---|---|
| January 17 | Feast of Ogun (Yoruba) |
| February 1 | Feast of Mama Brigitte |
| February 1 | Feast of Oya |
| March 17 | Feast of Damballah |
| March 20 | Feast of Legba Zaou |
| March 24 | Day of Blood |
| March 25 | Feast of Oshun |
| April 23 | Feast of Ogun (Santeria) |
| May 25 | Feast of Ochossi |
| June 16 | Death Anniversary of Marie Laveau |
| June 21 | Feast of Babalu Aye |
| July 2 | Feast of Expectant Mothers |
| July 16 | Feast of Ezili Danto |
| August 25 | Feast of Agasou |
| September 8 | Feast of Oshun |
| September 10 | Marie Laveau's birthday |
| September 24 | Feast of Obatala |
| September 29 | Feast of Eleggua |
| September 30 | Feast of Shango |

| | |
|---|---|
| October 4 | Feast of Orunmila |
| October 24 | Feast of Erinle |
| November 1-2 | Feast of the Dead |
| Full moon in November | Feast Day of Baba Yaga |
| November 25 | Feast of Oya |
| December 4 | Feast of Shango |
| December 10 | Feast of Ganga-Bois |
| December 17 | Feast of Babalu Aye |
| December 31 | Feast of Yemaya |

The Voodoo community has a lot of celebrations and events in store for its followers. These festivals and celebrations are among the ones they look forward to every year as those also allow them to show how they worship their deities, Lwas, and their Supreme God, Bondye.

# Conclusion

The Voodoo religion is a mystery for many, riddled with many secrets coupled with many spells, rituals, beliefs, traditions, and ceremonies that others may misunderstand. It does not have a world authority or a scripture. It centers more on community and supports each individual's experience, and responsibility, and empowerment.

Because of that, it is not surprising to hear and see many misconceptions about it, along with negative depictions. Fortunately, you have been given a chance to change that through this book, which aims to open your eyes to what Voodoo truly is. I hope it has helped you understand everything about Voodoo and understand how it embraces and covers every aspect of the human experience. With that, it is truly one of the most meaningful and valuable religions ever introduced to the world.

# Here's another book by Mari Silva that you might like

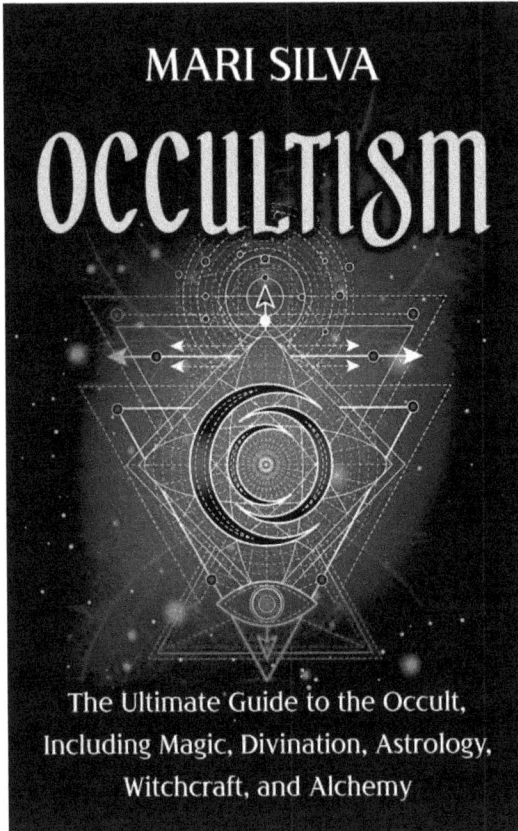

MARI SILVA

OCCULTISM

The Ultimate Guide to the Occult, Including Magic, Divination, Astrology, Witchcraft, and Alchemy

# Your Free Gift (only available for a limited time)

Thanks for getting this book! If you want to learn more about various spirituality topics, then join Mari Silva's community and get a free guided meditation MP3 for awakening your third eye. This guided meditation mp3 is designed to open and strengthen ones third eye so you can experience a higher state of consciousness. Simply visit the link below the image to get started.

https://spiritualityspot.com/meditation

# References

Admin. "Voodoo Magic Spells.Psychics Articles and History about Voodoo." Voodoo Magic Spells.Psychics Articles and History about Voodoo, 14 Jan. 2012,

magicvoodoospells.blogspot.com/2012/01/how-to-make-gris-gris.html.

Alvarado, Denise. "The Voodoo Hoodoo Spellbook: How to Make a Gris Gris Bag." The Voodoo Hoodoo Spellbook, 20 Dec. 2012, voodoohoodoospellbook.blogspot.com/2012/12/how-to-make-gris-gris-bag.html.

Alvarado, Denise M. "Ritual Symbols of the Voudou Spirits: Voudou Veves." Exemplore, Exemplore, 8 July 2008, exemplore.com/magic/voodooveves.

Beautiful, Tragic. "Simple Cleansing Spells." Tragic Beautiful, https://www.tragicbeautiful.com/blogs/style-blog/simple-cleansing-spells.

Coles, Donyae. "Creating Your Altar: A Beginner's Guide." Spiral Nature Magazine, 15 May 2017, www.spiralnature.com/spirituality/altar-beginners-guide/.

"Creating Shrines and Altars for Healing from Grief." GoodTherapy.org Therapy Blog, 31 Aug. 2011, www.goodtherapy.org/blog/shrine-altar-grief-healing/.

DHWTY. "The Origins of Voodoo, a Misunderstood Religion."
Www.ancient-Origins.net, www.ancient-origins.net/history-ancient-
traditions/origins-voodoo-002933.

"Everything about the Art of Witchcraft - Magickal Spot."
Magickalspot.com, magickalspot.com/.

Guilberly Louissaint. "What Is Haitian Voodoo?" The Conversation,
21 Aug. 2019, theconversation.com/what-is-haitian-voodoo-119621.

"Haiti: Introduction to Voodoo." Faculty.webster.edu,
faculty.webster.edu/corbetre/haiti/voodoo/overview.htm.

"HAITIAN VODOU, VODOU RELIGION, VOODOO &
VODOUN." Haitian Vodou, Voodoo, Las 21 Divisiones and Sanse,
ezilikonnen.com.

"Haitian Voodoo." Traveling Haiti, 13 Jan. 2016,
www.travelinghaiti.com/haitian-voodoo/.

HoodooWitch – Experiential Hoodoo Education for Everyone.
www.hoodoowitch.net/.

"How to Build an Ancestor Altar." Crescent City Conjure,
crescentcityconjure.us/blogs/city-of-conjure/how-to-build-an-ancestor-
altar.

"How to Do a House Blessing Spell for Protection & Cleansing."
Project Fey, https://www.projectfey.com/blogs/magical-
musings/6062912-how-to-do-a-house-blessing-spell-for-protection-
cleansing.

https://www.facebook.com/learn.religion. "Guide to the Beliefs and
Religions of the World." Learn Religions, 2018,
www.learnreligions.com/.

https://www.howstuffworks.com/tracy-v-wilson-author.htm. "How
Voodoo Works." HowStuffWorks, 16 Feb. 2007,
people.howstuffworks.com/voodoo.htm.

"Introduction to Voodoo - What Is Voodoo?" Wishbonix, 18 Feb.
2020, www.wishbonix.com/voodoo/

July 2015, Peter Moore | 17. "4 Intense Voodoo Festivals around the World." Wanderlust, www.wanderlust.co.uk/content/4-intense-voodoo-festivals-around-the-world/.

Kennon, Alexandra. "A Conversation with a High Priest of Vodou." Country Roads Magazine, 25 Sept. 2020, countryroadsmagazine.com/art-and-culture/people-places/the-truth-about-louisiana-voodoo-vodou/.

LaBorde, Lauren. "A Real Vodou Priestess on Cleansing Your Home of Evil Spirits and Negative Energy." Curbed New Orleans, 28 Oct. 2015, nola.curbed.com/2015/10/28/9906214/sallie-ann-glassman-home-cleanse-tips-voodoo.

Nana, Dr. "13 VOODOO SPELLS THAT ARE VERY POWERFUL and EFFECTIVE." Easy Spells, 9 Feb. 2020, lovespell.tips/13-vooodoo-spells-that-are-powerful-effective/.

Outpost, The. "Haitian Vodou: Summoning the Spirits | WilderUtopia.com." Www.wilderutopia.com, 30 Apr. 2013, www.wilderutopia.com/traditions/haitian-vodou-summoning-the-spirits/.

Refugiatei, Who made this site Design and Development Amy Marie Adams Arta. "James Duvalier." Jamesduvalier.com, jamesduvalier.com/history-beliefs-traditions-voodoo-part-haitian-vodou/

"Rituals, Traditions and Celebrations in Haiti." Usatoday.com, 2012, traveltips.usatoday.com/rituals-traditions-celebrations-haiti-103989.html.

"The Loa: Voodoo Spirits and How to Approach Them (for Witches)." Otherworldly Oracle, 18 Sept. 2019, otherworldlyoracle.com/loa-voodoo-spirits/.

The Voodoo Pantheon - Pagan. www.bellaonline.com/articles/art302082.asp.

Universe, Voodoo. "Creating Ancestor Altars in Santeria, Vodou, and Voodoo." Voodoo Universe, 23 Mar. 2014, www.patheos.com/blogs/voodoouniverse/2014/03/creating-ancestor-altars-in-santeria-vodou-and-voodoo/.

"Veve." Www.symbols.com, www.symbols.com/group/72/Veve.

"Voodoo - ReligionFacts." Religionfacts.com, religionfacts.com/voodoo.

"Voodoo - Rituals, World, Burial, Body, Life, Beliefs, Time, Person, Human." Deathreference.com, 2014, http://www.deathreference.com/Vi-Z/Voodoo.html.

"Voodoo Dolls." The Evil Wiki, evil.fandom.com/wiki/Voodoo_Dolls.

"Voodooria - an Authentic Voodoo Spell Casting Service." Voodooria, www.voodooria.com/.

"What Is the Doll?" Www.brown.edu, https://www.brown.edu/Departments/Joukowsky_Institute/courses/13t hings/7393.html